The Cus
Planner

The Marketing Series is one of the most comprehensive collections of books in marketing and sales available from the UK today.

Published by Butterworth–Heinemann on behalf of The Chartered Institute of Marketing, the series is divided into three distinct groups: *Student* (fulfilling the needs of those taking the Institute's certificate and diploma qualifications); *Professional Development* (for those on formal or self-study vocational training programmes); and *Practitioner* (presented in a more informal, motivating and highly practical manner for the busy marketer).

Formed in 1911, The Chartered Institute of Marketing is now the largest professional marketing management body in Europe with over 24,000 members and 28,000 students located worldwide. Its primary objectives are focused on the development of awareness and understanding of marketing throughout UK industry and commerce and in the raising of standards of professionalism in the education, training and practice of this key business discipline.

Books in the series

Computer Aided Marketing and Selling
Robert Shaw

The Creative Marketer
Simon Majaro

The Customer Service Planner
Martin Christopher

The Effective Advertiser
Tom Brannan

The Marketing Audit
Malcolm H. B. McDonald

The Marketing Planner
Malcolm H. B. McDonald

Marketing Strategy
Paul Fifield

The Customer Service Planner

Martin Christopher

**Published on behalf of
The Chartered Institute of Marketing**

BUTTERWORTH
HEINEMANN

Butterworth-Heinemann Ltd
Linacre House, Jordan Hill, Oxford OX2 8DP

 A member of the Reed Elsevier plc group

OXFORD   LONDON   BOSTON
MUNICH   NEW DELHI   SINGAPORE   SYDNEY
TOKYO   TORONTO   WELLINGTON

First published 1992
Paperback edition 1993
Reprinted 1994, 1995

British Library Cataloguing in Publication Data
Christopher, Martin
   The customer service planner – (The marketing
   series
   I. Title   II. Series
   658.8001

ISBN 0 7506 1710 1

Composition by Scribe Design, Gillingham, Kent
Printed and bound in Great Britain by Clays Ltd, St Ives plc

Contents

Preface

Over the last few years many books on customer service have been published and there can be no doubting that there is a totally different attitude towards customer service starting to emerge in many leading edge companies.

However, the problem that so many organizations still face is: how do we get started and what are the processes and systems necessary to sustain superior customer service in the marketplace?

It is to help address these issues that *The Customer Service Planner* has been constructed. It is not intended to be used as a book in the traditional sense and read from cover to cover – although some may care to do just that. Rather, it is hoped that the ideas and frameworks presented here will encourge creative thought and hence innovative actions by those who seek assistance in the customer service arena.

It will be apparent on using this Planner that the emphasis tends to veer towards distribution and logistics as the main drivers of service performance. The reason for this is because I have always felt that the key to success in customer service management is to strive to develop superior 'delivery systems' which are superior in the sense that they improve our customers' competitiveness and hence our own. There is substantial research evidence to support this viewpoint. For example, the PIMS studies (Profit Impact of Market Strategy), which draw upon a massive database, have shown that companies who are rated by their customers as superior to competitors on service achieve on average:

- 9 per cent higher prices.
- Twice the level of sales growth.
- 6 per cent increase in market share per year.

It is probably no exaggeration to say that in the closing years of the twentieth century and for some time beyond, customer service performance will be one of the most powerful marketing weapons that any organisation can deploy.

In putting *The Customer Service Planner* together I have derived great benefit from close association over the last twenty years with some of the leading thinkers and doers in the field of distribution, logistics and customer service. It is difficult to single out individuals when so many have contributed to the development of my ideas. However, there are three people on three different continents who have helped me shape my thoughts to a significant extent: Professor Douglas Lambert of the University of North Florida, USA, Dr John Gattorna of Gattorna

Strategy, Australia and Richard Yallop of Customer Service International Limited here in the UK. To these people, and to my secretary and personal assistant, Mrs Dorothy Hendry, who worked on the manuscript, I owe my thanks.

Martin Christopher
Professor of Marketing and Logistics Systems
Cranfield School of Management, UK

1 Rediscovering the customer

INTRODUCTION

Ever since the development and general acceptance in business of the marketing concept a great deal has been said and written about customers. Unfortunately much of the concern with customers has been at a superficial level and often more cosmetic than real. Organizations may talk about 'putting the customer at the centre of the business' but in reality they have few strategies or procedures for focusing the business around customer satisfaction.

The truth is that the majority of companies are still focused more on the products or services they manufacture or provide, rather than with the customers that they service.

In the traditional business everything from the organization structure to the budgeting and cost control system reinforces the over-riding concern with products and resources. Thus we find product managers but not market managers; or detailed accounting information on product profitability, but none on customer profitability and so on. *Yet the simple fact is that it is not the product that makes the profits but the customers.*

"There is only one valid definition of business purpose: to create a customer. It is the customer who determines what a business is.

What the business thinks it produces is not of first importance – especially not to the future of the business and to its success.

What the customer thinks he is buying and considers "*value*" is decisive – it determines what a business is, what it produces and whether it will prosper."

Peter Drucker
The Practice of Management
Butterworth-Heinemann, 1989

There is of course no doubt that the marketing environment has changed dramatically over the last ten years or so and these changes have substantial implications for how the business should address the customer. Specifically certain key environmental changes can be identified:

● A step change in customer expectations.
● A growing trend to commodity markets.
● A change in the balance of power from seller to buyer.
● The emergence of the service-sensitive customer.

CHANGING CUSTOMER EXPECTATIONS

There was a time – in most European economies it was the decade following the Second World War – when it was a sellers' market. Production was constrained, rationing was still widely in place, consumer disposable income was low and competition, and hence choice, was limited. In conditions such as these the question of service is peripheral and indeed such conditions tend to promote an attitude of 'take it or leave it' on the part of the supplier and a resigned acceptance from the buyer.

Thankfully that set of market conditions has now been reversed, certainly in the West and increasingly in the East. With the changed circumstances there has emerged a new, more demanding customer.

This customer, through experience and through the ability to make and exercise choices, has far greater expectations of the minimum acceptable level of product and service quality. At the same time there have been a handful of innovative companies who themselves, recognising the trend, have established higher levels of service and quality in their own 'offer' and hence have shown that they, the customer, do not have to put up with second best.

There is considerable evidence that customers vote with their feet.

● 96 per cent of dissatisfied customers never complain
  BUT
● 90 per cent of them will not return in the future
● ONE unhappy customer will tell at least NINE others
● 13 per cent of unhappy customers will tell at least twenty others

Source: USA White House
Office of Consumer Affairs

All the evidence points to a new breed of customer - and not only in consumer markets. The industrial buyer is much more sophisticated and is frequently subjecting his suppliers to formal evaluation. Thus it is now fairly common for a supplier to receive detailed analysis from a customer highlighting their on-time delivery performance, quality conformance, stock availability and so on.

The clear implication is that suppliers in any market who fall down on service and quality will not receive repeat business.

THE TREND TO COMMODITY MARKETS

One of the most pressing reasons why companies are increasingly reviewing their strategy towards customer service is that the strength of their brand names or corporate trademarks are no longer sufficient to differentiate the company from its competitors. There was a time in many markets when customers would specify a brand or supplier by name. However the situation so often encountered today is that customers are prepared to select any of a number of brands within a category.

Where competing products are seen to be similar or substitutable by customers then this is what is termed a *commodity market*.

Commodity markets are on the increase, particularly as technological or functional differences between competing brands or suppliers become less. Thus the purchaser of a TV set is less and less likely to be impressed by the claims that are made for the electronics contained within it since alternative brands will embody much the same technology.

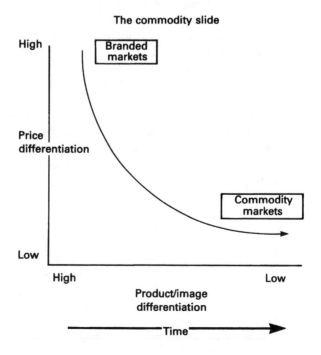

The commodity slide

The problem is that as brands slide down the 'commodity curve' the ability to command a premium price reduces and indeed we may find ourselves forced into price competition which itself will only tend to accelerate the slide because by reducing the price we are in effect saying: 'I cannot think of any other reason why you should buy my brand.'

The important message however is that this slide need not be inevitable. In fact there is growing evidence that quality and service can be a very powerful means of differentiation. In other words by the provision of superior service the organisation can make itself the supplier of choice - given of course that the product itself meets the requirements of the customer.

POWER CHANGES IN THE DISTRIBUTION CHANNEL

What seems to have happened since the end of the Second World War has been a gradual shift in the locus of power in most distribution channels away from the supplier and towards the buyer. This has occurred for a variety of reasons. Firstly competition as we have observed has increased, meaning that there is usually an alternative source of supply, and secondly the bargaining power of the buyer has grown because of the concentration that has occurred in many markets. A classic example of concentration of buying power is provided by the UK retail grocery business. The top two grocery retailers account for over 25 per cent of all the packaged food bought in Britain and the top 10 for almost 70%. Clearly this gives the major retailers substantial bargaining power – particularly since most of the purchase decisions are made centrally rather than at branch level.

One way in which this switch in the balance of power has manifested itself is in the growth in the demand of retailers for ever-higher levels of service, particularly in the area of delivery times and order completeness. Since the retailers' primary limiting factor is shelf space they have become increasingly aware of the need to boost their Return on Inventory Investment (ROII). One way in which this can be achieved is through requiring manufacturers to hold the stock and to make more frequent deliveries on a 'Just-in-Time' basis.

Improved stock-turn boosts return on capital

$$\text{Return on Inventory} = \underset{\uparrow}{\underset{\text{MARGIN}}{\frac{\text{PROFIT}}{\text{SALES}}}} \times \underset{\uparrow}{\underset{\text{STOCK-TURN}}{\frac{\text{SALES}}{\text{INVENTORY}}}}$$

The same move towards "Just-in-Time" as the basis for managing operations has taken place across most industries. The effect is the same: customers require higher levels of delivery service - particularly in the form of stock availability and delivery reliability, often within time windows of virtually two or three hours.

THE EMERGENCE OF THE SERVICE SENSITIVE CUSTOMER

In a sense all of the preceding trends have contributed to the emergence of a customer that places service and quality, in its broadest sense, ahead of all other factors when it comes to making a purchase decision.

We used to talk about the price sensitive customer and they still exist. However, survey after survey is indicating that the number one influence in the purchase decision, even ahead of price, is the expectation of the total quality (which includes service) that surrounds the offer.

This is not to suggest that price is unimportant but rather that the perception of higher quality and service enables a higher price to be charged.

This effect is easily demonstrated by using the economists' classic demand curve which suggests (Figure (i) in the diagram below) that as the price increases then the quantity demanded falls. By increasing the perception of quality and service the organisation in effect 'shifts the demand curve to the right' (Figure (ii) in the diagram below) thus implying that a higher price will not necessarily result in a fall in demand.

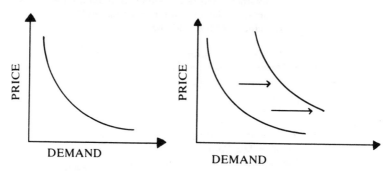

Figure (i) The Demand Curve   Figure (ii) The Impact of Superior Service and Quality

Evidence for this effect is provided by the so-called PIMS studies (Profit Impact of Market Strategy). After examining the marketing strategies of many thousands of companies the PIMS researchers concluded that one of the biggest contributors to profitability in any organization is the relative perceived quality of its products. In effect this enables those companies providing higher perceived quality to charge a higher price.

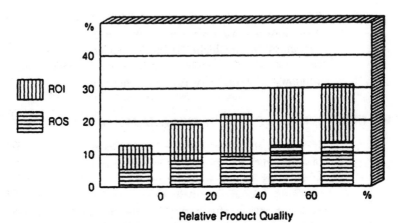

Relative product quality boosts rates of return

A recent study based upon a sample of over 1000 managers across 14 European countries showed that when it came to choice of supplier, quality and service issues came way ahead of price:

Rank	Item	Priority Index
1	Fitness for use (as perceived by the customer)	56
2	Problem solving (a systematic and committed effort to understand the true needs and difficulties of the customer)	48
3	Reliability ('A promise made is a promise kept')	47
4	After-sales service	44
5	Speed of delivery	43
6	Courtesy	31
7	Price	31

Source: John Humble
Service: *The Competitive Edge*
Management Centre Europe 1989

THE PRODUCT 'SURROUND'

Long before the current interest in customer service and quality improvement Theodore Levitt, perhaps one of the most perceptive of marketing commentators, was arguing that 'People don't buy products – they buy benefits'.

Behind this simple proposition is the fundamental notion that it is not so much what a product or service *is* that matters, but rather what it *does*. In other words: what impact on the customer in terms of *delivered values* does the product achieve? The classic, oft-quoted, example that Levitt provided was the manufacturer of the ¼" drill who always thought that people bought ¼" drills - whereas in fact what they bought was the promise of ¼" holes! This difference in definition is profoundly important because it focuses our minds on what people do with products and services and the perceived benefits they derive, rather than upon the intrinsic features of that product or service.

A useful way to visualise this concept is to think of the *offer* rather than the core product or service. The core is simply the basic assemblage of materials or features – the *tangibles* if you like. The total offer on the other hand is the sum of both the tangibles and the intangibles which continue to deliver benefits in the eyes of the customer. The figure below describes this concept of the core product which is enhanced by the product 'surround':

The total product concept

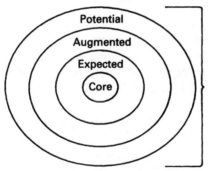

Total product is the sum of all four levels

Product level	Customer's view	Marketer's view	Personal computer example
Core product	Customer's generic need which must be met	Basic benefits which make product of interest	Data storage, processing, speed of processing, retrieval
Expected product	Customer's minimal set of expectations	Marketer's product decisions on tangible and intangible components\	Brand name, warranty service support, the computer shell
Augmented product	Seller's offering over and above what customer expects or is accustomed to	Marketer's other mix decisions on price, distribution, and promotion	Diagnostic software, trade-in allowance, base price plus options, dealer network. user clubs, personal selling
Potential product	Everything that potentially can be done with the product that is of utility to the customer	Marketer's actions to attract and hold customers regarding changed conditions or new applications	Use as a system controller, facsimile machine, music composer, and other areas of application

Source: B. Collins, Chapter 11 in D. Sampson (ed.), *Management for Engineers*, Longman Cheshire, 1989, p. 372.

The importance of this concept to our discussion here is that a major opportunity for enhancing the product surround, and hence for differentiating the product from its competitors, comes through customer service.

What do we mean by customer service? At its simplest, customer service can be defined as:

> *'a system organized to provide a continuing link between the time that the order is placed and the goods are received with the objective of satisfying customer needs on a long-term basis'.*

We shall need shortly to expand this definition but for the moment we can think of it as comprising three major components, which can themselves be further sub-divided:

● Pre-transaction service
● Transaction service
● Post-transaction service

Very simply the pre-transaction element of service refers to the systems, structures and environment which we seek to create before the sale takes place. The transaction components are those which the customer experiences during the sales process and the post-transaction refers to the after-sales context. In more detail these three elements comprise:

Customer service components

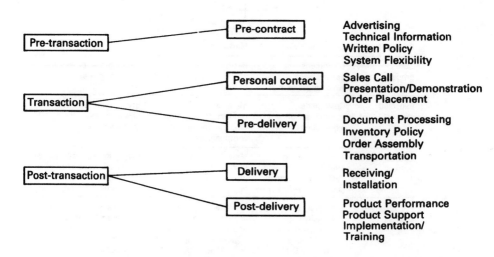

Sources: B.J. LaLonde & P.H. Zinszer, Customer Service Meaning and Measurement, NCPDM, Chicago, 1976 and J.P. Rakowski, "The Customer Service Concept", *Review of Business & Economic Research,* Vol 17, No. 2, Winter 1982

CUSTOMER RETENTION

One of the classic definitions of marketing is that it is concerned with 'getting and keeping customers'.

In practice if we look at where most organizations' marketing effort focuses, it is on the 'getting' of customers, rather than the 'keeping' of them. Thus an examination of the typical marketing plan will show a bias towards increasing market share rather than towards *customer retention*. Whilst new customers are always welcome in any business it has to be realized that an existing customer provides a higher profit contribution and has the potential to grow in terms of the value and frequency of purchases.

> It takes FIVE times as much effort, time and money to attract a new customer than it does to keep an existing customer
>
> *Source*: USA White House Office of Consumer Affairs

The importance of customer retention is underlined by the concept of the 'lifetime value' of a customer. The lifetime value of a customer is calculated as follows:

> AVERAGE TRANSACTION VALUE ×
> YEARLY FREQUENCY OF PURCHASE ×
> CUSTOMER "LIFE EXPECTANCY"
> = LIFETIME VALUE

One study of the car market in the USA found that a satisfied customer is likely to stay with the same supplier for a further twelve years after the first satisfactory purchase and during that period will buy four more cars of the same make. It is estimated that to a car manufacturer, this level of customer retention is worth $400 million in new car sales annually.

Domino's Pizzas, also in the USA, have calculated that good customer service is worth $5000 per customer! This is based upon a ten-year customer life. Hence all of Domino's Pizzas employees are aware of the fact that a single telephone order is not just for a $15 pizza - it is worth $5,000!

Rank Xerox use a measure of customer retention as part of a quarterly index of customer satisfaction that is used to determine bonuses and pay rises for management. Very simply the question they ask is: "How many of the customers that we had twelve months ago do we still have today?".

This measure is the real test of customer retention. It can be extended to look at the *value* of purchases made by the retained customer base to see how successful we have been in increasing the level of purchases from these accounts.

Customer retention indicators

(a)

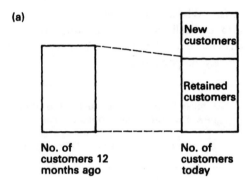

(b)

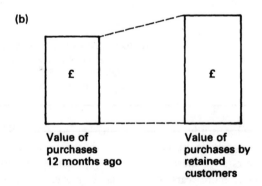

Rersearchers at Bain and Co, a management consulting company, have found that retained customers are more profitable than new customers for the following reasons:

Long term relationships with customers are more profitable for six reasons

- the cost of acquiring new customers can be substantial. A higher Retention Rate implies that fewer customers need be acquired and these can be acquired more cheaply;

- established customers tend to buy more;

- regular customers place frequent, consistent orders and, therefore, usually cost less to serve;

- satisfied customers often refer new customers to the supplier at virtually no cost;

- satisfied customers are often willing to pay premium prices for a supplier they know and trust;

- retaining customers makes market entry or share gain difficult for competitors.

Source: Bain & Company

A prime objective of any customer service strategy should be to enhance customer retention. Whilst customer service obviously also plays a role in winning new customers it is perhaps the most potent weapon in the marketing armoury for the keeping of customers.

There is rapidly emerging a new focus in marketing on the creation of 'relationships' with customers. The idea is that we should seek to create such a level of satisfaction with customers that they do not feel it necessary to consider alternative offers or suppliers. Many markets are characterized by a high level of volatility or 'promiscuity' amongst the customer base. In these markets customers will buy one brand on one occasion and then are just as likely to buy another on the next occasion.

The principle behind *Relationship Marketing* is that the organization should consciously strive to develop marketing strategies to maintain and strengthen customer loyalty. So, for example, an airline might develop a frequent flyer programme, or a credit card company might award points based upon the value of purchases made with the card that can then be redeemed for prizes. At the other extreme a company like IBM will seek to develop long-term relationships with its customers through training programmes, client seminars, frequent customer communication and so on.

The shift to relationship marketing

Transactions focus	Relationships focus
● orientation to single sales	● orientation to customer retention
● discontinuous customer contact	● continuous customer contact
● focus on product features	● focus on product benefits
● short time scale	● long time scale
● little emphasis on customer service	● high customer service emphasis
● limited commitment to meeting customer expectations	● high commitment to meeting customer expectations
● quality is the concern of production staff	● quality is the concern of all staff

Source: Relationship Marketing
Christopher, M.G. et al.
Butterworth-Heinemann, 1991

The logic of relationship marketing is well grounded. It is based upon the simple idea that if customers are satisfied with the totality of the offer, that is the core product and the service package that surrounds it, then they are unlikely to want to look for alternative sources of supply.

The combination of a superior product with a superior service package provides the ultimate source of sustainable competitive advantage.

2 The cost/benefit of customer service

All companies have to face a basic fact that there will be significant differences in profitability between customers. Not only do different customers buy different quantities of different products from us but the *cost to service* these customers will typically vary considerably.

The 80/20 rule will often be found to hold: that is 80 per cent of the profits of the business come from 20 per cent of the customers. Furthermore 80 per cent of the total costs to service will be generated from 20 per cent of the customers (but probably not the same 20 per cent!). Whilst the proportion may not be exactly 80/20 it will generally be in that region.

A typical graph of the distribution of customer profitability might be as below:

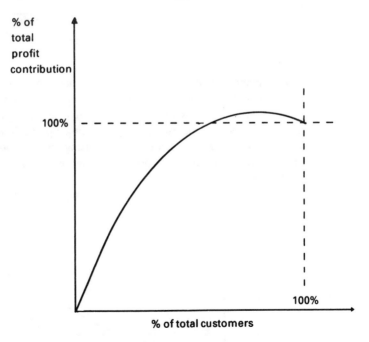

In this example it will be seen that there is a 'tail' of customers who are actually unprofitable and who therefore reduce total profit contribution!

The challenge to customer service management therefore is firstly to identify the real profitability of customers and then secondly to develop strategies for service that will improve the profitability of all customers. What has to be recognized is that there are costs as well as benefits in providing customer service and that the appropriate level and mix of service will need to vary by customer type.

The basic relationship between the level of service and the cost is often depicted as a steeply rising curve:

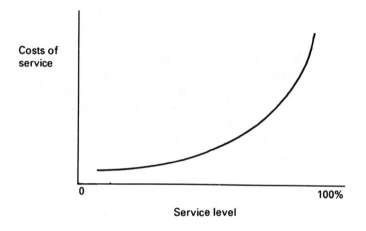

This phenomenon is largely due to the high costs of additional inventory required to cover against unexpectedly high levels of demand.

However if it is possible to find alternative service strategies for servicing customers, say for example by speeding up the flow of information about customer requirements and by using faster modes of transport, then the reduction in inventory costs may be such as to push the curve to the right.

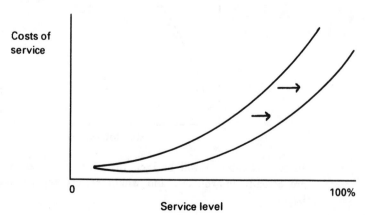

At the same time as the costs of service are being considered it is also appropriate to seek to understand what the *benefits* of service are. If improved levels of service cost more to achieve than they produce by way of long-term sales revenue then clearly those costs are not justified. Similarly it must also be recognised that different *segments* in the total market may respond in quite different ways to higher or lower levels of service.

Identifying customer response to service level changes is not easy. It is rather like trying to quantify the effects of advertising. Because there are so many variables impinging upon customer behaviour, including competitors' marketing activities, it would take a fairly complex experimental design to conduct rigorous empirical research into this issue. However what we are able to do through market research is to assess the *relative* sensitivity that different types of customer have to different aspects of service and these techniques will be addressed later in the book.

As far as the *absolute* level of service is concerned then clearly there must be a finite limit to the impact that service improvements can have upon customers' purchasing behaviour. In other words, after some point diminishing returns will set in. The diagram below makes this point:

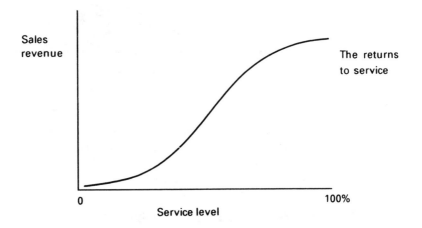

It is suggested that the service response is S-shaped for several reasons. Firstly in most markets there will be a minimum level of service that is deemed acceptable – this is the 'service threshold'. If we do not make it to this point then returns to additional service expenditure will be minimal. For example in a competitive retail market, offering to double stock availability from 5 to 10 per cent would clearly be ineffectual!

Once the threshold is passed increasing returns to service improvements should be achieved – if there is any degree of service sensitivity in the market. Inevitably, however, there will come a point where diminishing returns will set in - beyond this point we are in the region of service overkill where additional expenditure on service does not pay back.

Putting these two curves together highlights the nature of the cost/benefit trade-off in service level decisions:

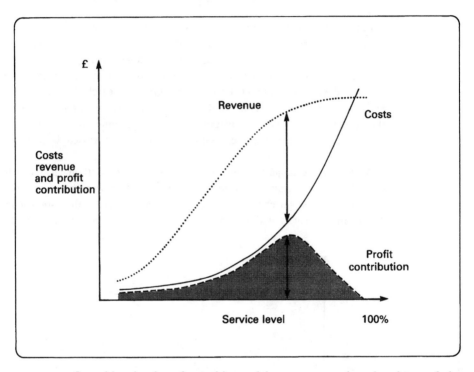

One thing is clear from this model: no matter what the shape of the service response curve or where the point of diminishing returns sets in, if the cost curve can be 'pushed to the right' then profits at all levels of service will be improved.

CUSTOMER PROFITABILITY ANALYSIS

As we have already indicated there will normally be an 80/20 relationship governing the profitability of customers. In other words 80 per cent of the total profit of the company will come from just 20 per cent of the customers.

Why should this be so?

The first observation is that different customers will often buy a different mix of products. Because individual products have different gross margins then clearly the mix of products purchased will impact upon the profitability of specific customers.

Beyond this however it must be recognized that there are also substantial differences in the costs of servicing individual customers. It has been said that "Profitability is largely determined by what happens *after* the point of production".

The Average Customer

"The significance of customer oriented costs is not their average value, but specifically how they vary by customer, by order size, by type of order and other key factors. Whilst the average cost per customer may be easily calculated, there may be no customer that incurs the average cost to serve. The need is to be aware of the customers at the extremes of the cost range because on the one hand, profits may be eroded by serving them and, on the other, although high profit is being generated, the business is vulnerable to competitive price-cutting. The table below shows an example of the range of values of some customer oriented costs expressed as a percentage of net sales. This illustrates how misleading the use of averages can be".

	Customer costs as a % of net sales		
	Low	Average	High
Order processing	0.2	2.6	7.4
Inventory carrying	1.1	2.6	10.2
Picking and shipping	0.3	0.7	2.5
Interplant freight & handling	0.0	1.5	7.6
Outbound freight	2.8	7.1	14.1
Commissions	2.4	3.1	4.4

Source: G.V. Hill & D.V. Harland
'The Customer Profit Centre'
Focus Vol 2. No. 2 1983

The costs of service begin with the order itself - what time does the salesperson spend with the customer; is there a key account manager whose time is spent wholly or in part working with that customer; what commissions do we pay on those sales?

Then there are the order processing costs which themselves will differ according to the number of lines on the order, the number of orders and their complexity. Beyond this there will be transport costs, materials handling costs and often inventory and warehousing costs - particularly if the products are held on a dedicated basis for customers, e.g. as with own-label products.

With many customers it will often be the case that the supplying company is allocating specific funds for customer promotions, advertising support, additional discounts and the like. In the case of promotions (e.g. a special pack for a particular retailer) there will most likely be additional hidden costs to the supplier. For example the disruption to production schedules and the additional inventory holding cost is rarely accounted for and assigned to customers.

The basic principle of customer profitability analysis is that the supplier should seek to assign all costs that are specific to individual accounts. A useful test to apply when looking at these costs is to ask the question: "What costs would I *avoid* if I didn't do business with this customer?"

The benefit of using the principle of 'avoidability' is that many costs of servicing customers are actually shared amongst several or many customers. The warehouse is a good example – unless the supplier could release warehousing space for other purposes then it would be incorrect to allocate a proportion of the total warehousing costs to a particular customer.

A checklist of costs to include when drawing up the 'profit and loss account' for specific customers is given below:

The customer profit and loss account

Revenues   Net sales value

Less

Costs

(attributable costs only)

- Cost of sales (actual product mix)
- Commissions
- Sales calls
- Key account management time
- Trade bonuses and special discount
- Order processing costs
- Promotional costs (visible & hidden)
- Merchandising costs
- Non-standard packaging/unitization
- Dedicated inventory holding costs
- Dedicated warehouse space
- Materials handling costs
- Transport costs
- Documentation/communications costs
- Returns/refusals
- Trade credit (actual payment period)

Whilst it may not be practicable to undertake such an analysis for individual accounts it should be possible to select representative customers on a sample basis so that a view can be gained of the relative costs associated with different types of accounts or distribution channels or even market segments.

The recommended procedure for implementing customer profitability analysis is highlighted in the flowchart:

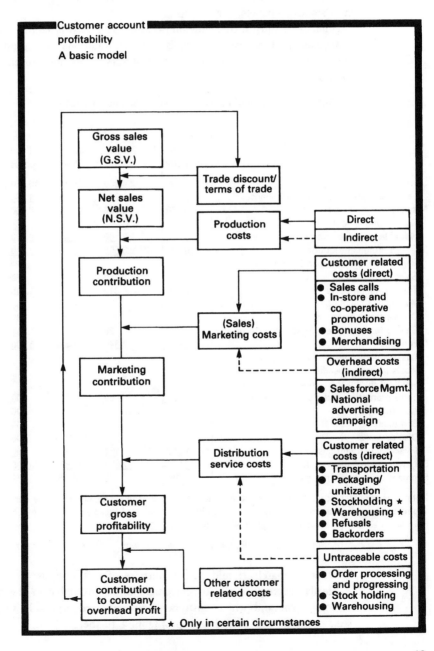

Customer account profitability
A basic model

★ Only in certain circumstances

What will often emerge from these studies is that the largest customers in terms of volume?, or even revenue, may not be the most profitable because of their high costs of service. Thus it may be that the larger customers gain larger volume-based discounts, they require more frequent deliveries to more dispersed locations and they may insist on non-standard pallets, for example.

The cases illustrated below show how the real profitability of different customer types can be disguised under traditional accounting and is only brought to light when the costs of service are introduced into the analysis:

Profitability by type of account: a contribution approach ($000)

	Total Company	Department Stores	Grocery Chains	Drug Stores	Discount Stores
		Type of Account			
Sales	$42,500	$6,250	$10,500	$19,750	$6,000
Less discounts, returns and allowances	2,500	250	500	1,750	=
Net sales	40,000	6,000	10,000	18,000	6,000
Cost of goods sold					
(variable manufacturing costs)	20,000	2,500	4,800	9,200	3,500
Manufacturing contribution	20,000	3,500	5,200	8,800	2,500
Variable selling and distribution costs:					
Sales commissions	800	120	200	360	120
Transportation costs	2,500	310	225	1,795	170
Warehouse handling	600	150	–	450	–
Order-processing costs	400	60	35	280	25
Charge for investment in accounts receivable	700	20	50	615	15
Contribution	15,000	2,840	4,690	5,300	2,170
Assignable nonvariable costs (costs incurred specifically for the segment during the period)					
Sales promotion and slotting allowances	1,250	60	620	400	170
Advertising	500	–	–	500	–
Bad debts	300	–	–	300	–
Display racks	200	–	–	200	–
Inventory carrying costs	1,250	150	200	800	100
Segment controllable margin	$11,500	$2,630	$3,870	$3,100	$1,900
Segment controllable margin-to-sales ratio	27.1%	42.1%	36.9%	15.7%	31.7%

Note: This approach could be modified to include a charge for the assets employed by each of the segments, as well as a deduction for the change in market value of these assets. The result would be referred to as the net segment margin (residual income).

Source: Stock, J. R., Lambert, D. M., *Strategic Logistics Management*. Irwin 1987

What ultimately should be the purpose of this analysis?

Ideally we require all our customers to be profitable in the medium to long term and where customers currently are profitable we should seek to build and extend that profitability further.

The customer profitability matrix illustrated below provides some generalized guidance for strategic direction.

Net
sales
value
of
customer
account

Hi

Lo

Lo

Hi

Cost of service

	PROTECT	COST ENGINEER
	BUILD	DANGER ZONE

Customer
profitability
matrix

Briefly the appropriate strategies for each quadrant of the matrix are:

Build These customers are relatively cheap to service but their net sales value is low. Can volume be increased without a proportionate increase in the costs of service? Can our sales team be directed to seek to influence these customers' purchases towards a more profitable sales mix?

Danger Zone These customers should be looked at very carefully. Is there any medium to long-term prospect either of improving net sales value or of reducing the costs of service? Is there a strategic reason for keeping them? Do we need them for their volume even if their profit contribution is low?

Cost Engineer These customers could be more profitable if the costs of servicing them could be reduced. Is there any scope for increasing drop sizes? Can deliveries be consolidated? If new accounts in the same geographic area were developed would it make delivery more economic? Is there a cheaper way of gathering orders from these customers, e.g. tele-sales?

Protect The high net sales value customers who are relatively cheap to service are worth their weight in gold. The strategy for these customers should be to seek relationships which make the customer less likely to want to seek alternative suppliers. At the same time we should constantly seek opportunities to develop the volume of business that we do with these whilst keeping strict control of costs.

Ideally the organization should seek to develop an accounting system that would routinely collect and analyse data on customer profitability. Unfortunately most accounting systems are *product* focused rather than *customer* focused. Likewise cost reporting is traditionally on a *functional* basis rather than a *transactional* basis. So for example we know the costs of the transport function as a whole or of making a particular product. What we do not know though, are the costs of delivering a specific mix of product to a particular customer.

There is a pressing need for companies to move towards a system of accounting for customers and marketing as well as accounting for products. As we have previously observed it is customers who make profits, not products!

3 Developing a customer service strategy

If customer service is to play a significant role in the organisation's marketing mix programme then it must be planned and managed just as any other marketing element such as price or promotion.

In the same way that the company develops a product strategy or an advertising strategy so too it must develop a customer service strategy.

The classic approach to strategic planning can provide a framework for creating a customer service strategy:

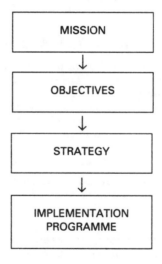

Essentially this approach requires the definition of the service mission of the business – an overall vision of what role service should play in the culture and shared values of the business, followed by a clear definition of the precise service objectives, particularly as they relate to the overall marketing mix of the company. The strategy then is essentially the mechanisms by which these objectives will be achieved and the implementation programme is the step-by-step plan for putting the service package into action.

1. THE SERVICE MISSION

The idea of the 'Mission Statement' is now widely accepted in business. Ideally a corporate mission statement should be an expression of the *vision*, the *culture* and the *shared values* of the organisation as well as defining the boundaries or *scope* of the business. In practice we find that so many mission statements are 'motherhood' statements – in other words they tend to be loose, woolly and non-specific but, perhaps, create a warm feeling in the reader.

To have real value a corporate mission statement should clearly provide guidance and direction but, beyond this, it should also focus upon the unique and distinctive elements of its offer. It has been said that to have validity it should not be possible to remove the company's name from the mission statement and replace it with another's and for it still to make sense.

WORLDWIDE MISSION STATEMENT

DHL will become the acknowledged global leader in the express delivery of documents and packages. Leadership will be achieved by establishing the industry standards of excellence for quality of service and by maintaining the lowest cost position relative to our service commitment in all markets of the world.

Achievement of the mission requires:

☐ Absolute dedication to understanding and fulfilling our customers' needs with the appropriate mix of service, reliability, products and price for each customer.

☐ An environment that rewards achievement, enthusiasm, and team spirit and which offers each person in DHL superior opportunities for personal development and growth.

☐ A state of the art worldwide information network for customer billing, tracking, tracing and management information/communications.

☐ Allocation of resources consistent with the recognition that we are one worldwide business.

☐ A professional organisation able to maintain local initiative and local decision making while working together within a centrally managed network.

The evolution of our business into new services, markets, or products will be completely driven by our single-minded commitment to anticipating and meeting the changing needs of our customers.

Perhaps the most important function that a mission statement can provide is to underline the service dimension of the organisation's intended strategic positioning. A good example is that provided by DHL Worldwide Express, one of the world's largest and most successful express delivery companies.

The process of defining the mission statement will itself be a valuable exercise, obviously involving the top management of the organization but also preferably drawing upon the views of those who will be responsible for the development of detailed implementation programmes. The last thing any company needs is another set of platitudes, issued from the top, embodying fine-sounding rhetoric but which does not carry commitment at any level.

Albrecht and Zemke have summarized the prerequisites for a meaningful mission statement:

Requirements for a successful service mission

1. It is nontrivial; it has weight. It must be more than simply a "motherhood" statement or slogan. It must be reasonably concrete and action-oriented.
2. It must convey a concept or a mission which people in the organization can understand, relate to, and somehow put into action.
3. It must offer or relate to a critical benefit premise that is important to the customer. It must focus on something the customer is willing to pay for.
4. It must differentiate the organization in some meaningful way from its competitors in the eyes of the customer.
5. If at all possible, it should be simple, unitary, easy to put into words, and easy to explain to the customer.

Source: Karl Albrecht & Ron Zemke
Service America, Dow-Jones Irwin 1985

One word of caution: the service mission statement should be a living thing, it needs to be reviewed periodically and adjusted to reflect the changes in the marketing environment and the company's response to that environment.

2. CUSTOMER SERVICE OBJECTIVES

Objectives are goals and must be clearly defined and understood if effective strategies are to be developed. In the words of the old adage: "If you don't know where you're going, any road will get you there"!

In the context of customer service there are certain questions that need to be answered before objectives can sensibly be set:

● How important is customer service compared to the other elements in the marketing mix i.e. product, price or promotional variables?
● Which aspects of customer service contribute most to overall customer satisfaction and market share?
● What dimensions of service are seen as priorities by customers when they make their choice of suppliers?

A considerable body of research now exists which points to the importance of service variables in the purchase decision across a wide range of products and industries. The following chart summarizes the general conclusions of much of this research.

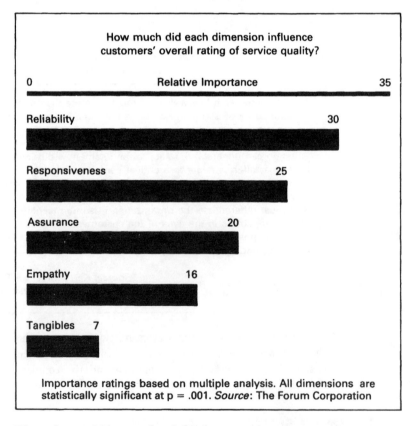

How much did each dimension influence customers' overall rating of service quality?

0	Relative Importance	35

Reliability 30

Responsiveness 25

Assurance 20

Empathy 16

Tangibles 7

Importance ratings based on multiple analysis. All dimensions are statistically significant at p = .001. *Source*: The Forum Corporation

These five variables can be defined as:

- *Reliability* – ability to perform the promised service dependably, accurately and consistently. This means doing it right, over a period of time.

- *Responsiveness* – prompt service and willingness to help customers. Speed and flexibility are involved here.

- *Assurance* – knowledge and courtesy of staff and their ability to inspire trust and confidence.

- *Empathy* – caring individualized attention to customers.

- *Tangibles* – physical facilities, equipment, staff appearance, i.e. the physical evidence of the service which conveys both functional and symbolic meaning.

Source: Parasuraman, A., et al: 'SERVQUAL: A Multiple Item Scale for Measuring Consumer Preferences of Service Quality" *Journal of Retailing.* Vol 64. No 1, 1988

From this it will be seen that reliability and responsiveness are quite clearly the key variables. However it is important that all five elements should be structured into the definition of customer service objectives. To assist in this process of definition it is helpful to think of the role that customer service plays at each step in the purchase process. For convenience these steps might be characterized using our earlier model:

- The Pre-transaction stage
- The Transaction stage
- The Post-transaction stage

At each stage in the process from the first contact with the potential customer through to the sale and any after-sales support it is important to establish precisely defined objectives for each element of the service mix. The listing below gives an indication of the level of detail that is required:

The components of customer service

Pre-transaction elements

For example:

- Written customer service policy
  (Is it communicated internally or externally, is it understood, is it specific and quantified where possible?)
- Accessibility
  (Are we easy to contact/do business with? Is there a single point of contact?)

- Organization structure
  (Is there a customer service management structure in place? What level of control do they have over their service process?)
- System flexibility
  (Can we adapt our service delivery systems to meet particular customer needs?)

Transaction elements

For example:

- Order cycle time
  ((What is the elapsed time from order to delivery? What is the reliability/variation?)
- Inventory availability
  (What percentage of demand for each item can be met from stock?)
- Order fill rate
  (What proportion of orders are completely filled within the stated lead-time?)
- Order status information
  (How long does it take us to respond to a query with the required information? Do we inform the customer of problems or do they contact us?)

Post-transaction elements

For example:

- Availability of spares
  (What are the in-stock levels of service parts?)
- Call out time
  (How long does it take for the engineer to arrive and what is the "first call fix rate"?)
- Product tracing/warranty
  (Can we identify the location of individual products once purchased? Can we maintain/extend the warranty to customers' expected levels?)
- Customer complaints, claims etc.
  (How promptly do we deal with complaints and returns? Do we measure customer satisfaction with our response?)

Ultimately however, the primary objective of any customer service strategy can be expressed very simply – *to reduce the customer's costs of ownership.*

In other words for service to provide real value to the customer it must in some way make the transaction more 'profitable'. Thus for example, delivery twice a week instead of once a week reduces the customer's average inventory by half and therefore cuts the cost of carrying inventory by half. Again, reliable on-time delivery means that the customer can reduce the need to carry safety stock, again resulting in a cut in the inventory holding costs. Electronic Data Interchange (EDI) can reduce the customer's ordering costs, assured quality can eliminate the need for in-bound inspection and so on.

Put simply, service represents a shift in costs from customer to supplier and as such, properly managed, this can become a major source of competitive advantage.

One of the best examples of how this concept is being put to work in practice comes from the revolutionary approach to purchasing decisions that many of the world's leading retailers are using. This is the technique known as Direct Product Profitability – or more simply 'DPP'.

The idea behind DPP is that in many transactions the customer will incur costs other than the immediate purchase price of the product. Sometimes these costs can be hidden and often they can be substantial – certainly big enough to reduce or even eliminate net profit in the case of a retailer. Since DPP has been primarily used in the retail industry (although the principle has a much wider currency) we will explain the concept in the context of retail business.

Firstly, a definition of DPP:

Direct Product Profit is a measure of an item's actual contribution to profit. DPP addresses the measure of profit at a point beyond the traditional gross margin calculation by:

● Adjusting the gross margin for each item to reflect deals, allowances, net forward buy income, prompt payment, discounts etc.

● Identifying and measuring the costs that can be directly attributed to individual products (direct product costs like labour, space, inventory and transport).

The box below describes the steps in moving from a crude gross margin measure to a more precise DPP.

Direct Product Profit (DPP)

The net profit contribution from the sale of a product after allowances are added and all costs that can be rationally allocated or assigned to an individual product are subtracted

	Sales
–	Cost of goods sold
=	Gross margin
+	Allowances and discounts
=	Adjusted gross margin
–	Warehouse costs
	Labour (labour model – case, cube, weight)
	Occupancy (space and cube)
	Inventory (average inventory)
–	Transportation costs (cube)
–	Retail costs
	Stocking labour
	Front end labour
	Occupancy
	Inventory
=	Direct product profit

Because the product characteristics and associated costs vary so much item by item (e.g. cube, weight, case pack count, handling costs, space occupied, turnover) the retailer needs to look at DPP at the item level. Similarly, because shelf space is the limiting factor for the retailer the key measure of performance becomes DPP/Square Metre.

Some examples of how DPP/Square Metre can differ dramatically from simple gross margin are shown below for different products moving through a specific retailer's own distribution system:

Gross margin does not predict profit			
	Gross margin	DPP	Average DPP/Sq.Metre
	%	%	$
Baby food	11	3.4	0.11
Beans and rice	11	3.9	0.24
Shortening and oil	11	7.3	0.98
Paper products	19	7.2	0.47
Cake mix	19	10.1	0.44
Jelly and jam	22	16.7	1.01
Household cleaners	24	17.3	1.05
Ice cream	23	6.2	0.99
Butter	10	4.6	1.97
Frozen vegetables	34	23.1	2.60
Cigarettes	12	13.2	6.56
Dentifrice	31	18.6	1.42
Facial tissues	15	–	(0.01)

The importance to the supplier of all this is based upon the previously stated objective of customer service strategy as being 'to reduce the customer's costs of ownership'. In other words the supplier should be looking at his products and asking the question: How can I favourably influence the DPP of my customers by changing either the characteristics of the products I sell or the way I distribute them?

From pack design onwards there are a number of elements that the manufacturer or supplier may be able to vary in order to influence DPP/Square Metre in a positive way:

Ways to impact the retailer's DPP

● Change product/pack design
● Change case size
● Examine alternatives to traditional shipping units e.g. pallets
● Increase delivery frequency
● Offer merchandising/price marking facility
● Direct store deliveries

In setting customer service objectives there is a fundamental requirement to understand the nature of the customer's cost base and then seek to explore ways in which a superior service package can be developed. Ultimately, we have suggested, the objective of any customer service strategy should be to reduce the customer's costs of ownership.

3. CUSTOMER SERVICE STRATEGY

Only rarely are markets homogeneous, with similar needs, requirements and preferences. Instead what usually exists is a number of sub-markets or segments which share similar characteristics within a total market, but will quite likely differ considerably in those characteristics from other segments. Thus a classic marketing strategy is to target a limited number of segments and to design specific marketing mix programmes for each segment.

The same principle applies to *service segmentation*: not all our customers require the same type or level of service.

Thus a very powerful device for achieving a more cost-effective expenditure of the service pound or dollar is to identify the extent to which different service groups with distinct service needs exist in the market. By understanding the service segmentation of the market we are better able to target service and indeed to design appropriate 'service packages'.

A systematic approach to the development of a service strategy based upon segmentation is detailed below. Essentially it follows a four step process:

A framework for customer service strategy

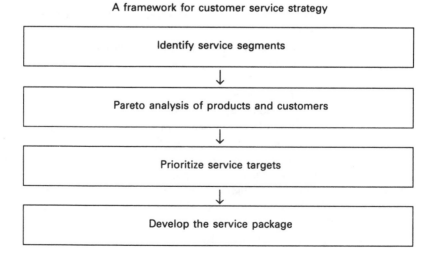

31

Step 1. Identify service segments

Markets can be segmented in many different ways. However the basic question is: "What are the key dimensions that influence buyer behaviour and how do they differ by segment?" Another way of expressing this is to ask: "What are the 'order-winning criteria' for this customer group compared to another?" In other words, what do we have to do well in order to become a preferred supplier to this segment?

The answers to these questions can easily be ascertained through market research. The first requirement is to identify the key service variables that decision-makers use when evaluating suppliers. The technique we favour here is an 'elicitation' approach whereby a small representative sample of buyers are asked indirectly to provide the salient or 'top-of-the-head' reasons why one supplier is different from another, or superior or inferior to another.

The first point to emphasize is that customer service is *perceptual*. Whatever our own "hard" internal measures of service might say our service performance is, perceptions are the reality. We might use measures which, whilst providing useful measures of productivity, do not actually reflect the things the customer values. For example whilst "stock availability" is a widespread internal measure of performance, a more appropriate external measure from the customer's viewpoint could be "on-time delivery". Hence it is critical that we develop a set of service criteria that are meaningful to customers.

The approach to service segmentation suggested here follows a three-stage process:

1 Identify the key components of customer service as seen by customers themselves.
2 Establish the relative importance of those service components to customers.
3 Identify 'clusters' of customers according to similarity of service preferences.

1. Identifying the key components of customer service

It is a common fault in marketing to fail to realize that customers do not always attach the same importance to product attributes as the vendor. The same principle applies to customer service. Which aspects of service are rated most highly by the customer? If a supplier places its emphasis upon stock availability, but the customer regards delivery reliability more highly, it may not be allocating its resources in a way likely to maximize sales. Alternatively a company that realizes that its customers place a higher value on completeness of orders than they do on, say, regular scheduled deliveries could develop this knowledge to its advantage.

Therefore it is important to understand the factors that influence buyer behaviour and, in the context of customer service, which particular elements are seen by the customer to be the most important.

The first step in research of this type is to identify the relative source of influence upon the purchase decision. If, for example, we are selling components to a manufacturer, who will make the decision on the source of supply? This is not always an easy question to answer as in many cases there will be several people involved. The purchasing manager of the company to which we are selling may only be acting as an agent for others within the firm. In other cases his influence will be much greater. Alternatively if we are manufacturing products for sale through retail outlets, is the decision to stock made centrally by a retail chain or by individual store managers? The answers can often be supplied by the sales force. The sales representative should know from experience who are the decision makers.

Given that a clear indication of the source of decision-making power can be gained the customer service researcher at least knows who to research. The question remains as to which elements of the vendor's total marketing offering have what effect upon the purchase decision.

Ideally once the decision-making unit in a specific market has been identified an initial, small-scale research programme should be initiated based upon personal interviews with a representative sample of buyers. The purpose of these interviews is to elicit, in the language of the customers, firstly the importance they attach to customer service *vis-à-vis* the other marketing mix elements such as price, product quality, promotion etc., and secondly, the specific importance they attach to the individual components of customer service.

The importance of this initial step in measuring customer service is that relevant and meaningful measures of customer service are generated by the customers themselves. Once these dimensions are defined we can identify the relative importance of each one and the extent to which different types of customer are prepared to trade-off one aspect of service for another.

2. Establishing the relative importance of customer service components
One of the simplest ways of discovering the importance a customer attaches to each element of customer service is to take the components generated by means of the process described in Step 1 and to ask a representative sample of customers to rank order them from the 'most important' to the 'least important'. In practice this is difficult, particularly with a large number of components and would not give any insight into the relative importance of each element. Alternatively a form of rating scale could be used. For example, the respondents could be asked to place a weight from 1 to 10 against each component according to

how much importance they attached to each element. The problem here is that respondents will tend to rate most of the components as highly important, especially since those components were generated on the grounds of importance to customers anyway. A partial solution is to ask the respondent to allocate a total of 100 points amongst all the elements listed, according to perceived importance. However, this is a fairly daunting task for the respondent and can often result in an arbitrary allocation.

Fortunately a relatively recent innovation in consumer research technology now enables us to evaluate very simply the implicit importance that a customer attaches to the separate elements of customer service. The technique is based around the concept of trade-off and can best be illustrated by an example from everyday life. In considering, say, the purchase of a new car we might desire specific attributes, e.g. performance in terms of speed, and acceleration economy in terms of petrol consumption, size in terms of passenger and luggage capacity and, of course, low price. However, it is unlikely that any one car will meet all of these requirements so we are forced to trade-off one or more of these attributes against the others.

The same is true of the customer faced with alternative options of distribution service. The buyer might be prepared to sacrifice a day or two on lead-time in order to gain delivery reliability, or to trade-off order completeness against improvements in order entry etc. Essentially the trade-off technique works by presenting the respondent with feasible combinations of customer service elements and asking for a rank order of preference for those combinations.

Let us take a simple example where a respondent is asked to choose between different levels of stock availability, order cycle time and delivery reliability. For the sake of example the following options are presented:

Stock availability	:	75 per cent
		85 per cent
		95 per cent
Order cycle time	:	2 days
		3 days
		4 days
Delivery reliability	:	± 1 day
	:	± 3 days

The various trade-offs can be placed before the respondent as a series of matrices:

		Order cycle time		
		2 days	3 days	4 days
	75%			9
Stock	85%			
availability	95%	1		

		Order cycle time		
		2 days	3 days	4 days
Delivery	± 1 day	1		
reliability	± 3 days			6

		Stock availability		
		75%	85%	95%
Delivery	± 1 day			1
reliability	± 3 days	6		

The idea is that the respondent should complete each matrix to illustrate his/her preference for service alternatives. Thus, with the first trade-off matrix between order cycle time and stock availability, it is presumed that the most preferred combination would be an order cycle time of two days with a stock availability of 95 per cent and the least preferred combination an order cycle time of five days with a stock availability of 75 per cent. But what about the other combinations? Here the respondent is asked to complete the matrix to show his/her own preferences. An example of a typical response is given below:

		Order cycle time		
		2 days	3 days	4 days
	75%	6	8	9
Stock	85%	3	5	7
availability	95%	1	2	4

		Order cycle time		
		2 days	3 days	4 days
Delivery	± 1 day	1	3	5
reliability	± 3 days	2	4	6

		Stock availability		
		75%	85%	95%
Delivery	± 1 day	4	2	1
reliability	± 3 days	6	5	3

Using computer analysis the implicit "importance weights" that underlie the initial preference rankings can be generated. For the data in the
above example the following weights emerge:

Service element		Importance weight
1 Stock availability	75%	− 0.480
	85%	0
	95%	+ 0.480
2 Delivery time	2 days	+ 0.456
	3 days	0
	4 days	− 0.456
3 Delivery reliability	± 1 day	+ 0.239
	± 3 days	− 0.239

Thus for this respondent stock availability would appear to be marginally
more important than delivery time and both were in the region of twice
as important as delivery reliability. Information such as this can be most
useful. It can tell us, for example, that in this hypothetical case, a stock
availability of 85 per cent with 2 days' delivery and a reliability of ± 1
day is seen as being equally acceptable as a 95 per cent availability with
2 days' delivery and ± 3 days' reliability (a combined weight of 0.695
compared with 0.697). This suggests that a tightening up on reliability
might reduce stockholding and still provide an acceptable level of
customer service.

3. Identifying customer service segments
Now that we have determined the importance attached by different
respondents to each of the service attributes previously identified, the
final step is to see if any similarities of preference emerge. If one group
of respondents for example have a clearly distinct set of priorities than
another then it would be reasonable to think of them both as different
service segments.

How can these customer service segments be identified? One technique
that has been successfully used in this connection is Cluster Analysis.
Cluster Analysis is a computer-based method for looking across a set of
data and seeking to 'match' respondents across as many dimensions as
possible. Thus if two respondents completed the stage 2 trade-off matrices in a very similar way their importance scores on the various service
dimensions would be similar and hence the Cluster Analysis would assign
them to the same group.

A recent study in a fast moving consumer goods market found that
there were two distinct service segments, one group placed major

emphasis upon delivery variables such as on-time delivery, frequency of delivery and completeness of order – this was labelled the 'Just-in-Time' segment. The other segment placed greater emphasis upon close liaison with the supplier, quality of communications and ease of ordering., As a result of this study the supplying company knew where to focus its resources by customer type to much greater effect.

Step 2. Pareto analysis

The Pareto, or 80/20 Rule, has already been described. It can provide us with the basis for developing a more cost-effective service strategy.- Fundamentally, the issue is simply that since not all our customers are equally profitable nor are our products equally profitable, should not the highest service be given to key customers and to key products? Since we can assume that money spent on service is a scarce resource then we should look upon the service decision as a resource allocation issue.

It will be recalled that the Pareto curve takes on the following general shape:

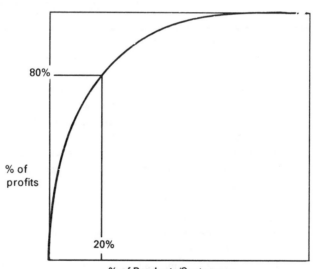

% of Products/Customers

We can further sub-divide the curve so that we have three categories: The top 20 per cent of products and customers by profitability are the 'A' category; the next 30 per cent or so are labelled 'B' and the final 50 per cent are category 'C'. The precise split between the categories is arbitrary as the precise distribution will vary from business to business and from market to market.

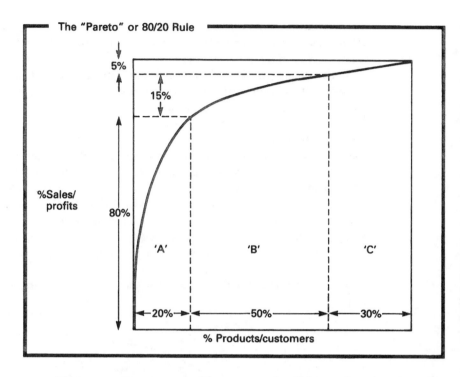

The "Pareto" or 80/20 Rule

The appropriate measure of importance should be profit rather than sales revenue or volume. The reason for this is that revenue and volume measures might disguise considerable variation in costs. In the case of customers this cost is the 'cost to serve' and we have already explored the suggested approach to measuring customer profitability. In the case of product profitability we must also be careful that we are identifying the appropriate service-related costs as they differ by product. One of the problems here is that conventional accounting methods do not help in the identification of these costs. Typically accounting systems will focus upon factory costs and will use some method of full-cost allocation to deal with the problem of fixed costs.

Our preferred approach to product profitability analysis is based upon measuring the costs that attach to a product as it moves through the logistics system. Sometimes these costing methods have been referred to as *Throughput Accounting* and *Activity Based Costing*.

The basic principle is that we should identify and manage the activities that produce the costs rather than the costs *per se*.

This principle is not dissimilar to the idea of Direct Product Profitability (DPP) that we discussed earlier.

What we should be concerned to do at this stage in the analysis is to identify the *contribution* to profit that each product (at the individual stock-keeping unit (SKU) level) makes. By contribution we mean the difference between total revenue accruing and the directly attributable costs that attach as the product moves through the logistics system.

Given that we can develop reasonable estimates of profit for individual customers and products, to what use should it be put?

Step 3. Prioritize service targets
Looking first at differences in product profitability, what use might be made of the A,B,C, categorization? Firstly it can be used as the basis for classic inventory control whereby the highest level of service (as represented by safety stock) is provided for the 'A' products, a slightly lower level for the 'B' products and lower still for the 'C's'. Thus we might seek to follow the stockholding policy shown below:

Product category	Stock availability
A	99%
B	97%
C	90%

Alternatively, and probably to be preferred, we might differentiate the stockholding by holding the 'A' items as close as possible to the customer and the 'B' and 'C' items further back up the supply chain. The savings in stockholding costs achieved by consolidating the 'B' and 'C' items as a result of holding them at fewer locations would normally cover the additional cost of despatching them to the customer by a faster means of transportation (e.g. overnight delivery).

Perhaps the best way to manage product service levels is to take into account both the profit contribution *and* the individual product stock-turn.

Stock-turn is measured as:

$$\frac{\text{Annual sales}}{\text{Average annual inventory}}$$

We can bring both these measures together in the form of a simple matrix:

		Lo	Hi
Stock-turn (by SKU)	Hi	(1) Seek cost reductions	(2) Provide high availability
	Lo	(3) Review	(4) J.I.T. delivery

Profit contribution (by SKU)

Quadrant 1. Seek cost reductions
Because these products have high stock-turn it would suggest that they are in frequent demand. However they are also low in profit contribution and the priority should be to re-examine their costs – particularly on an Activity Cost basis – to see if there is any scope for enhancing profit.

Quadrant 2. Provide high availability
These products are frequently demanded and they are more profitable. We should offer the highest level of service on these items by holding them as close to the customer as possible and with high availability (e.g. 99per cent plus). Because there will be relatively few of these items we can afford to follow such a strategy.

Quadrant 3. Review
Products in this category should be regularly appraised with a view to deletion from the range. They do not contribute to profits (or at least only marginally) and they are slow movers from a sales point of view. Unless they play a strategic role in the product portfolio of the firm then there is probably a strong case for dropping them.

Quadrant 4. J.I.T. delivery
Because these products are highly profitable but only sell at a relatively slow rate they are candidates for J.I.T. delivery. In other words they should be kept in some central location, as far back up the supply chain as possible in order to reduce the total inventory investment, and then shipped by express transport direct to customers.

This concept of service prioritization can be extended to include customer priorities. Because the same 80/20 rule applies to customers as it does to products, it makes sense to focus resources on *key accounts* and *key products*.

The diagram below shows that if the 80/20 rule applies both to products and customers then all businesses are actually very dependent upon a very few customers buying a few high profit lines. Indeed the arithmetic is easy:

20 per cent of customers buying 20 per cent of the products
= 4 per cent of all customer/product transactions

Which provides

80 per cent of 80 per cent of total profit = 64 per cent

In other words just 4 per cent of transactions (measured order-line by order-line) give us 64 per cent of all our profit!

Customer service and the '80/20 Rule'

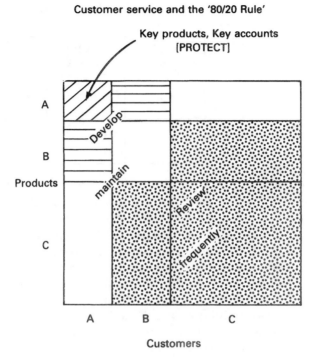

Customers

How can we make use of this important fact? The first thing is obviously to offer the highest levels of service and availability to key customers ordering key products. At the other end of the spectrum we should constantly review the less profitable customers and the less profitable products. In between there is scope for a degree of pragmatism perhaps based upon the service priority matrix illustrated below. Here customers

Service priority matrix

		Product class		
		A	B	C
Customer class	I	1	2	6
	II	3	4	7
	III	5	8	9

Priority standards

Priority range	Stock level standard	Delivery standard
1–3	100%	48 hours
4–6	97%	72 hours
7–9	90%	120 hours

are classified by profitability (I, II, & III) and similarly so are products (A, B, C). Then, using judgement, priorities (1–9) are assigned. At the same time differential targets are set for stock availability and delivery. Clearly as shown here it is a fairly crude system but it is capable of being tailored to meet specific needs.

One variation on this theme is to take into account the 'critical value' of an item to the customer. This is particularly relevant when developing a service strategy for spare parts. The idea is that if certain items are essential for, say, the operation of a machine where the down-time costs are high then those parts would be accorded a high critical value. If appropriate a 'weight' could be assigned on the basis of criticality and the 80/20 ranking based on profit could be adjusted accordingly. The table below provides an example:

Critical value analysis

Products	Profitability rank order	Critical value to customers 1	2	3	Rank X critical value	Order of priority for service
C	1			X	3	1
P	2		X		4	2 =
R	3		X		6	5
B	4	X			4	2 =
X	5	X			5	4
Y	6			X	18	8
Z	7		X		14	7
H	8	X			8	6
J	9			X	27	10
K	10		X		20	9

Critical values: 1 = Sale lost
2 = Slight delay acceptable
3 = Longer delay acceptable

Step 4. Develop the service package

To compete effectively in any market requires the ability to develop some differential advantage over competing companies and their product or service offerings. Sometimes this differential advantage may be in terms of distinctive product attributes or related benefits as perceived by the customer. On other occasions it may be price or, alternatively, the product may be promoted in such a way that it acquires a distinctive image in the eyes of the market. In just the same way, customer service can be used to develop a differential advantage and indeed there can be a major benefit to the company in using customer service in this way. For example in competitive markets where real product differentiation may be difficult to establish and where to compete on price would only lead to profit erosion, it makes sense to switch the marketing emphasis to customer service.

Clearly this implies that we should stress those components of the total customer service mix which have the greatest impact on the buyer's perception of us as a supplier. This thinking needs to be carried right through into the design of the customer service offering. This offering can best be described as the customer service 'package', for it will most likely contain more than one component.

The design of the package will need to take account of the differing needs of different market segments so that the resource allocated to customer service can be used in the most cost-effective way. Too often a uniform, blanket approach to service is adopted by companies which does not distinguish between the real requirements of different customer types. This can lead to customers being offered too little service or too much. The precise composition of the customer service package for any market segment will depend on the results of the market research described previously. It will also be determined by budgetary and cost constraints and this is where the trade-off analysis previously described can be helpful. If alternative packages can be identified which seem to be equally acceptable to the buyer it makes sense to choose the least cost alternative. For example, it may be possible to identify a customer service package with high acceptability which enables the emphasis to be switched away from a high level of inventory availability towards, say, improved customer communication.

Once a cost-effective package has been identified in this way it should become a major part of the company's marketing mix – 'using service to sell' is the message here. If the market segments we serve are sensitive to service, then the service package must be actively promoted. One way in which this can be achieved with great effect is by stressing the impact on the *customer's* costs of the improved service package, e.g. what improved reliability will do for his own stock planning, what shorter lead-times will do for his inventory levels, how improved ordering and invoicing systems will lead to fewer errors and so on. All too often the customer will not appreciate the impact that improved service offered by the supplier can have on his, the customer's, bottom line.

Beyond the simple presentation of a marketing message based around an improved customer service package lies the opportunity to develop tailor-made service offerings, particularly to key accounts, based upon 'negotiated' service levels. The idea here is that no two customers are alike, either in terms of their requirements or, specifically, in terms of their profitability to the supplier. One UK-based company in the consumer electronics field identified that whilst three of its major customers were roughly equivalent in terms of their annual sales value there were considerable differences in the costs generated by each. For example one customer required delivery to each of its 300-plus retail outlets, whilst the other took delivery at one central warehouse. Similarly one company paid within 30 days of receiving the invoice, the others took nearer to 40 days to pay. Again, one of the three was found to place twice as many 'emergency' orders as the others. Careful analysis of the true costs showed that the profitability of the three customers differed by over 20 per cent yet each customer received the same value-related discounts and the same level of customer service!

4 Monitoring and controlling customer service strategy

"If you can't measure it, you can't manage it"

Effective management of customer service requires a systematic and continuing focus on measurement and control. Like any process when left to its own devices, the customer service system will ultimately decay. It is important therefore that appropriate measures be identified for controlling the customer service process.

The analogy with quality control in manufacturing is a good one. Whilst in the past the emphasis on quality control was on inspection of the output, now it is on control of the process. The idea is very simple: if the process is under control then the quality of the output is guaranteed, indeed the need for inspection of the final product disappears. We now recognise that we can never 'inspect quality' into a product. In other words if all we do is measure the output of a process and reject

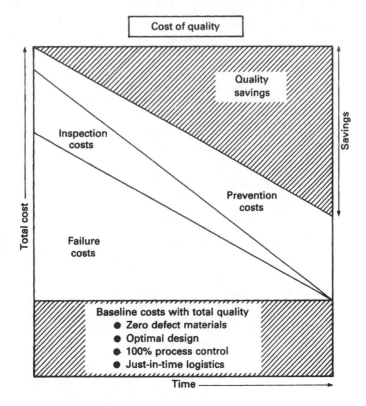

failures it implies that we are prepared to accept a certain proportion of non-quality events.

In today's environment this is no longer acceptable. In fact it can be demonstrated that quality failures are so costly, either in terms of customer relations or the cost of putting things right, that improvements in quality actually save money, or indeed make money. This is the meaning of the phrase 'quality is free'. The diagram on page 45 shows just how the cost of quality is comprised:

Many companies have little idea what the hidden costs of non-conformance to customer quality requirements are. The table below shows how it is possible for the Cost of Quality (COQ) to exceed 20 per cent of a typical company's total revenue – enough in some cases to eliminate all profit!

Cost of quality in ABC company

The following are a few examples (high, medium and low) of over 150 identified activities.

Activity	£K	Category
1. Surplus inventory costs (over JIT levels)	6400	ER
2. Obsolete inventory costs – write off	5600	IF
3. Absenteeism (8%)	3753	IF
4. Loss of existing customers	2800	LO
5. Production scrap	2733	IF
6. Product inspection	1764	AP
7. Purchase price excess	1286	IF
8. Loss of premium pricing margins	855	LO
9. Correcting product design drawings	765	IF
10. Unwanted labour turnover/retraining (4%)	732	IF
11. Unused product features	600	ER
12. Sales invoice errors/excess receivables	600	EF
13. Goods receiving inspection	576	AP
14. Product warranty/liability	522	EF
15. Rework of defective products	315	IF
16. Correcting production tooling errors	260	IF
17. Quality system planning/audit	144	PR
18. Expediting parts from suppliers	144	AP
19. Correcting sales orders	122	IF
20. Quality consultant's review	116	PR
21. Employee training	112	PR
22. Analysis of product failure in the field	105	EF
23. Purchase order amendments	32	IF
24. Revised operating plan	19	IF
Total COQ	**30355**	

Summary	£K		
PR Prevention	372		
AP Appraisal	2484		
IF Internal failure	15617		
EF External failure	1227	Sales revenue	132600
ER Exceeding reqts.	7000	COQ %	22.9
LO Lost opportunities	3655		

Source: Quality Costing & Competitive Benchmarking
J.D. Hackett, CIM Institute, Cranfield, 1990

Clearly improving the quality of service therefore will be beneficial not only to the customer but will also reduce the suppliers' costs. In other words the possibility of enhancing competitive advantage through the quality of service is a goal well worth pursuing.

SERVICE AS A PROCESS

As we have noted there is a direct analogy between quality management in manufacturing and quality management in customer service.

The key to success in quality improvement is not to rely on inspection of the output of the process but rather to control the process itself. Imagine that this process is a 'pipeline' that begins with suppliers, runs through our own business (whether it involves manufacturing or any form of value-adding activity) through intermediaries and on to customers. To ensure that customer satisfaction is achieved at the end of the pipeline requires that everything that happens in the pipeline must be carefully monitored and controlled.

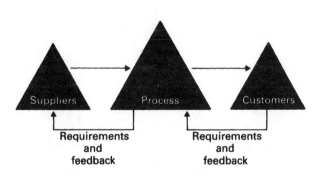

The pipeline from suppliers to customers

The first step in managing the service pipeline is to understand the structure of the process. Unlike in oil pipelines the network of materials and information flows, activities and procedures that link suppliers with end users, is complex. A recommended approach to defining the pipeline structure is to *flow chart* the steps along the chain that begins with a customer's order and ends with delivery. A greatly simplified example is shown on page 48. The detailed flow chart from which this summary was taken covered a very large sheet of paper!

The next step is to identify the critical points where if something goes wrong then the entire process will be affected – for instance a stock-out in the warehouse or a failure to meet a production plan. These critical points are where process control must be applied.

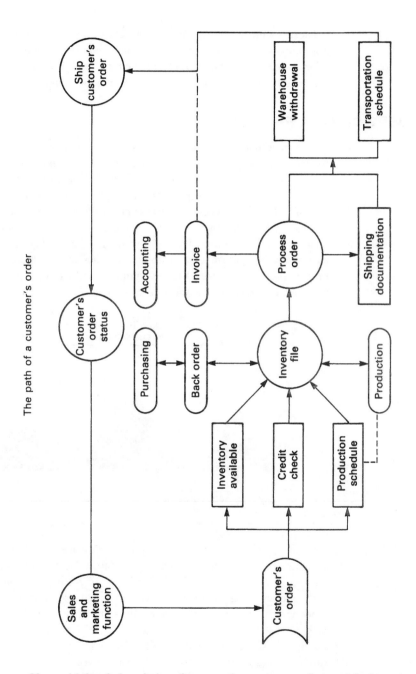

The path of a customer's order

If we think of the chain of events from source of material through to the end user as a series of supplier-customer relationships then it will become clear that what we are advocating is a control of *service levels* at each of the supplier-customer interfaces.

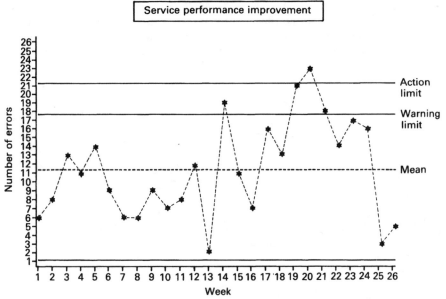

Testing for stablity: Statistical Control Chart for picking errors in the warehouse

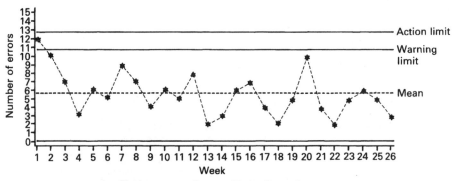

Picking errors: Process Under Control

It is not sufficient however that we merely control the process but rather we must improve the process so that action limits are not transgressed and that, as in the example above, the mean performance level is improved. Ideally we should seek to 'fail-safe' the system so that things cannot go wrong because of automatic checks and procedures. This is the system that the Japanese call 'Poka-Yoke'.

In seeking to identify the causes of failure or error a technique that is growing in popularity is 'cause and effect' analysis, making use of a 'Fishbone Diagram'. The idea is that we should look at all the possible causes of a problem and then analyse the causes themselves to seek out the possible explanations. The example below shows how process improvement can be greatly assisted by such a technique:

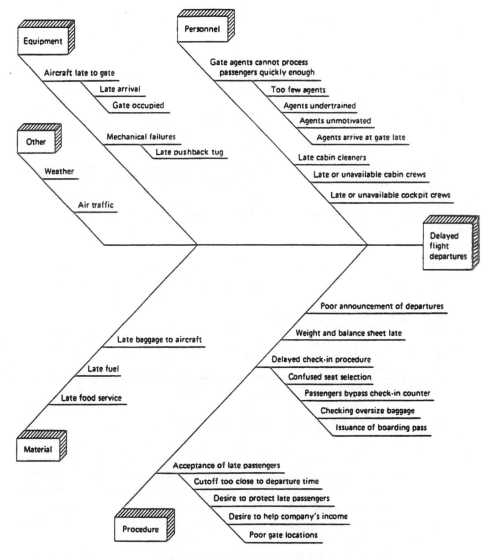

Causes of Flight Departure Delays

Source: Daryl Wyckhoff, "New Tools for Achieving Service Quality," *Cornell Hotel and Restaurant Administration Quarterly* (November 1984), 78–91.

A useful device for going beyond symptoms and really identifying root causes is the device of 'Asking why five times'. A striking example is provided by Taiichi Ohno, one of the gurus of Japanese manufacturing and quality service management:

'Asking *why* five times'

1. Q. *Why* did the machine stop?
   A. There was an overload and the fuse blew.

2. Q. *Why* was there an overload?
   A. The bearing was not sufficiently lubricated

3. Q. *Why* was it not lubricated sufficiently?
   A. The lubrication pump was not pumping sufficiently.

4. Q. *Why* was it not pumping sufficiently?
   A. The shaft of the pump was worn and rattling.

5. Q. *Why* was the shaft worn?
   A. There was no strainer and metal scrap got in.

Repeating *Why*? five times, like this, can help uncover the root problem and correct it. If this procedure were not carried through, one might simply replace the fuse or the pump shaft. In that case, the problem would recur within a few months.

Taiichi Ohno
Toyota Production System

SETTING SERVICE STANDARDS

Obviously if service performance is to be controlled then it must be against pre-determined standards.

Ultimately the only standard to be achieved is 100 per cent conformity to customer expectations. This requires a clear and objective understanding of the customers' requirements and at the same time places an obligation upon the supplier to shape those expectations. In other words there must be a complete match between what the customer expects and what we are willing and able to provide. This may require *negotiation* of service standards since clearly it is in neither party's interest to provide service levels which would lead to a long-term deterioration in profitability – either for the supplier or the customer.

What are the customer service elements for which standards should be set?

Firstly there are the *internal service standards* to which we have already referred. In many respects they mirror the standards that our *external* customers place upon us. As far as these external standards are concerned they must be *defined by the customers themselves*. This requires customer research and competitive benchmarking studies to be conducted and these are explored fully later in this section.

However for the moment we can indicate some of the key areas where standards are essential:

Customer service elements

- Order cycle time
- Stock availability
- Order-size constraints
- Ordering convenience
- Frequency of delivery
- Delivery reliability
- Documentation quality
- Claims procedure
- Order completeness
- Technical support
- Order status information

Let us examine each of these in turn:

Order cycle time	This is the elapsed time from customer order to delivery. Standards should be defined against customer's stated requirements.
Stock availability	This relates to the percentage of demand for a given line item (Stock Keeping Unit, or SKU) that can be met from available inventory.
Order-size constraints	More and more customers seek 'Just-in-Time' deliveries of small quantities. Do we have the flexibility to cope with the range of customer demands likely to be placed upon us?
Ordering convenience	Are we accessible and easy to do business with? How are we seen from the customers' viewpoint? Do our systems talk to their systems?
Frequency of delivery	A further manifestation of the move to 'Just-in-Time' is that customers require more frequent deliveries within closely specified time-windows. Again it is flexibility of response that should be the basis for the performance standard.

Delivery reliability	What proportion of total orders are delivered on time? It is a reflection not just of delivery performance but also of stock availability and order processing performance.
Documentation quality	What is the error rate on invoices, delivery notes and other customer communications? Is the documentation 'user friendly'? A surprisingly large number of service failures are from this source.
Claims procedure	What is the trend in claims? What are their causes? How quickly do we deal with complaints and claims? Do we have procedures for 'service recovery'?
Order completeness	What proportion of orders do we deliver complete, i.e. no back-orders or part shipments?
Technical support	What support do we provide customers after the sale? If appropriate do we have standards for call-out time and first time fix rate on repairs?
Order status information	Can we inform customers at any time on the status of their order? Do we have 'hot lines' or their equivalent? Do we have procedures for informing customers of potential problems on stock availability or delivery?

All of these issues are capable of quantification and measurement against customer requirements. Similarly they are all capable of comparison against competitive performance.

Whilst all these elements of customer service are of potential importance, two in particular are increasingly seen as being crucial to winning and keeping customers: Delivery Reliability and Order Completeness. In fact these two elements can be combined into a single performance measure: On-time Order Fill.

The measure is expressed as a ratio:

$$\text{On-time order fill} = \frac{\text{Orders delivered complete on customer's specified date}}{\text{All orders delivered}}$$

It must be recognized that from the customer's perspective there are only two levels of service – either 100 per cent or 0 per cent. In other words either the customer gets exactly what he/she ordered at the time and place required or they don't. It must also be remembered that 100 per cent order fill rates are extremely difficult to achieve – the laws of probability see to that! If there are 10 items on a particular order and each item is carried in stock at the 95 per cent level of availability then the probability that the complete order can be filled is 0.95^{10} which is 0.599. In other words, just over a 50/50 chance that we can satisfy the complete order.

The table below shows how the probability of order fill diminishes as the number of items on the customer order increases:

Probability of a complete order				
Number of lines in order	Line item fill rate			
	90%	92%	94%	95%
1	.900	.920	.940	.950
2	.810	.846	.884	.903
3	.729	.779	.831	.857
4	.656	.716	.781	.815
5	.590	.659	.734	.774
6	.531	.606	.690	.735
7	.478	.558	.648	.698
8	.430	.513	.610	.663
9	.387	.472	.573	.630
10	.348	.434	.538	.599
11	.314	.339	.506	.569
12	.282	.368	.476	.540
13	.254	.338	.447	.513
14	.225	.311	.400	.488
15	.206	.286	.395	.463
16	.185	.263	.372	.440
17	.167	.243	.349	.418
18	.150	.223	.328	.397
19	.135	.205	.309	.377
20	.122	.185	.290	.358

Ideally organizations should establish standards and monitor performance across a range of customer service measures. For example, using the pre-transaction, transaction and post-transaction framework, the following measures provide valuable indicators of performance:

Pre-transaction	Stock availability
	Target delivery dates
	Response times to queries
Transaction	Order fill rate
	On-time delivery
	Back orders by age
	Shipment delays
	Product substitutions
Post-transaction	First call fix rate
	Customer complaints
	Returns/Claims
	Invoice errors
	Service parts availability

It is possible to produce a composite index based upon multiple service measures and this can be a useful management tool particularly for communicating service performance internally. Such an index is shown below where the weight attached to each service element reflects the importance that the customers attach to those elements:

Composite service index			
Service element	Importance weight (i)	Performance level (ii)	Weighted score (i) x (ii)
Order fill rate	30%	70%	.21
On-time delivery	25%	60%	.15
Order accuracy	25%	80%	.20
Invoice accuracy	10%	90%	.09
Returns	10%	95%	.095
		Index =	0.745

Clearly in constructing such indices it is crucial that objective measures of the importance of each service element be obtained. The only valid source of this information is through some form of customer service survey and the Trade-Off Analysis technique described in Chapter 3 is an ideal device for establishing importance weights.

CUSTOMER SERVICE SURVEYS AND COMPETITIVE BENCHMARKING

So far our discussion of performance measurement has focused upon 'hard' measures of service like stock availability. However, as was noted earlier in the book, it should always be borne in mind that *customer service is perceptual.* In other words the ultimate measure of performance is how the customer sees us. Ideally therefore the customer service-oriented company needs to monitor these perceptions, market segment by market segment and also where possible, measure the customers' perceptions of the company's performance against other suppliers. This is the concept of *competitive benchmarking.*

The process of benchmarking service performance comprises four steps:

THE COMPETITIVE BENCHMARKING PROCESS

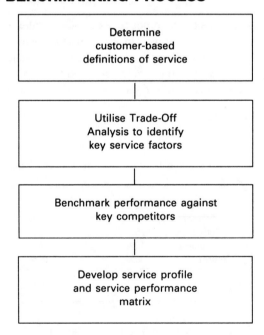

We have already described the first two steps in Chapter 3 when discussing the possibilities for service segmentation. The same approach to eliciting customers' own definitions of service and using trade-off analysis to discern the relative importance of each service element can be used to great effect here. The idea is to establish a limited number of key *service factors* that can be monitored on a regular basis against competition.

These first two steps can usually be accomplished using relatively small samples and in effect they could serve as a 'pilot' study to provide the basis for a larger scale survey of the company's customers.

This wider survey can often be achieved by means of a postal questionnaire, the sample for which should be chosen to reflect the different types of customer. The main purpose of the questionnaire is to present the components of service as elicited in Step 1 and to ask the respondents to rate the company and its competitors on each of these elements in terms of their perceived performance. The table below reproduces part of a typical questionnaire for use in service benchmarking. For each competing company in that market the respondent is asked to rate its performance on each of the relevant dimensions of service identified in Step 1. When the responses are aggregated by trade sector or market segment, patterns may well emerge. On each customer service element it is possible to see how each competing supplier compares in terms of each other.

Other analysis can include regional breakdowns and analyses by size and type of customer. The usual statistical tests can be applied to identify if different scores on any dimensions have significance. To ensure an unbiased response to the questionnaire it is preferable if the survey can be carried out anonymously or via a third party such as a market research agency. Also, as in Steps 1 and 2, it is important to make sure that the people to whom the questionnaire is sent represent the decision-making structure within their concerns.

Management now has a customer service database upon which it can make a number of crucial decisions regarding the design of more cost-effective customer service policies.

Customer service benchmark questionnaire					
How would you rate ABC on the following: (Score from 1 to 5; 1 = very poor, 5 = excellent) *Please circle*					
Order cycle time	1	2	3	4	5
Stock availability	1	2	3	4	5
Order size constraints	1	2	3	4	5
Ordering convenience	1	2	3	4	5
Frequency of delivery	1	2	3	4	5
Delivery reliability	1	2	3	4	5
Quality of documentation	1	2	3	4	5
Claims procedure	1	2	3	4	5
Order completeness	1	2	3	4	5
Technical support	1	2	3	4	5
Order status information	1	2	3	4	5

Analysis of the data will then enable service profiles for each company to be constructed and again this data can be presented alongside the importance ranking identified from the earlier trade-off analysis.

Customer service profile

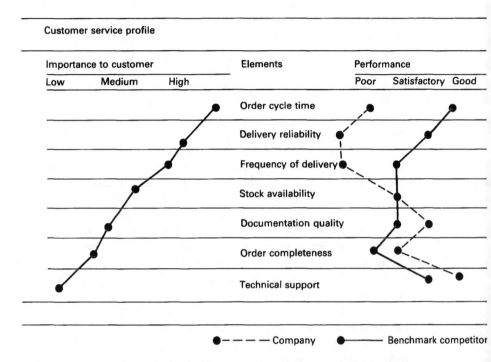

Importance to customer			Elements	Performance		
Low	Medium	High		Poor	Satisfactory	Good

Order cycle time

Delivery reliability

Frequency of delivery

Stock availability

Documentation quality

Order completeness

Technical support

●– – – – Company   ●——— Benchmark competitor

Further profiles can be produced by dis-aggregating the data by customer type, market segment, region, etc. Competitive service profiles can provide additional insights if non-users or lapsed customers are also included in the survey. Companies who have conducted these types of competitive analyses find that they provide a clear guide for action. Often competitive profiles point to weaknesses that had not previously been recognized. Additional benefit can be derived from repeating these studies on a regular basis to monitor changes and trends.

COMPARING SERVICE PERFORMANCE WITH CUSTOMERS' SERVICE PRIORITIES

Using the data generated from these surveys, we are in a position to contrast two key findings: firstly what are the important dimensions of service and secondly how well is the company perceived to perform on those key dimensions?

A simple way of displaying this data is to represent the findings in the form of a Service Performance Matrix. On one axis we measure the importance rating (usually on a scale of 1 to 5) and on the second axis is shown the actual perceived performance rating (also on a 1 to 5 scale). The figure below shows such a matrix.

The Service Performance Matrix

Importance to customer
(I = unimportant; 5 = highly important)

		1	2	3	4	5
	1					
Perceived performance	2				*1	
(I = poor	3		*2			*4
5 = Excellent)	4			*3		
	5	*5	*6			

Key: * Service attributes 1–6

In this hypothetical example we have shown the scores on five dimensions jointly for importance and perceived performance. The five dimensions might be taken to be:

1   Order cycle time
2   Order completeness
3   Documentation quality (e.g. invoices)
4   Delivery reliability
5   Technical support
6   Sales visits

The interpretation of this matrix is simple. It is clearly crucial that the company be seen to be performing well in those service dimensions that the customer deems to be important. Conversely it can be argued that if the service dimension is seen to be less important to the customer then high performance on that dimension amounts to 'service overkill' or a misuse of resources.

Thus in this example the company appears to be underperforming on dimensions 1 and 4 – order cycle time and delivery reliability – and possibly over-performing on 5 – technical support and 6 – sales visits. The diagram below generalizes this point.

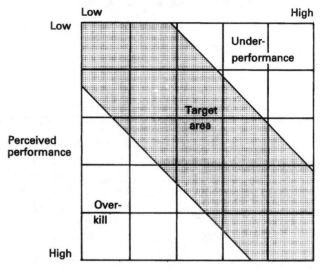

Customer service management indicators

Importance to customers

Similar charts can be produced for individual market segments, sales areas, distribution channels or whatever by further analysis of the data emerging from the customer service audit.

The analysis can be further extended by including competitive performance data. Thus the 'perceived performance' scale is modified to show 'relative' performance. In other words we express our performance as perceived by customers as a ratio of competitors' perceived performance. The figure below shows such a modified analysis in the form of a matrix:

Competitive position matrix

		Competitive disadvantage	Competitive parity	Competitive advantage
	5	1* Major weakness	4*	Major strength
Importance				3*
		6* Minor weakness	2*	Minor strength *5
	1			

| | 0.2 | 0.5 | 1.5 | 5.0 |

Relative performance

Key: * 1–6 Service attributes

Three broad strategic positions emerge from this analysis:

1 *Competitive advantage*
Major strength (high importance, high relative performance).
Minor strength (low importance, high relative performance).

2 *Competitive parity*
Weaknesses and strengths match those of the competition.

3 *Competitive disadvantage*
Major weakness (high importance, low relative performance).
Minor weakness (low importance, low relative performance).

In the hypothetical example depicted above, the company appears to have a major weakness in its order cycle time (1) and a minor weakness on sales visits (6). It has a potential advantage with the quality of its documentation (3) and its technical support (5) to a lesser extent. It has competitive parity on (4) and (2) – delivery reliability and order completeness.

Whilst the preceding example related to a manufacturer supplying a distributor or stockist, exactly the same procedure could be applied to a consumer or service market. Thus in designing a competitive service package for an airport hotel, say, research could be conducted on similar lines. In such an instance it might be useful to begin with a focus group representative of the target market, say business travellers, and then to use the service criteria generated through that means as the basis for more detailed customer research.

The key point to remember in measuring and monitoring customer service performance is that the metric, or 'measuring rod' used must be customer relevant and normally that means that the measures must be generated directly from customers through research. A common mistake is to design customer service studies using *internally* derived standards (i.e. determined by management) and thus as a result, possibly drawing misleading conclusions.

BENCHMARK THE PROCESS, NOT JUST THE OUTPUTS

It will be recalled that earlier in this chapter we stressed the importance of managing the *process* if the required standard of *output* was to be achieved. Similarly, an extension of the benchmarking concept is to conduct competitive and non-competitive comparisons of service processes.

The idea behind this is that much can be learned from how other companies manage their service systems. These companies need not be competitors, in fact it may be difficult to gain access to the details of competitors' processes. Rather the companies we should be examining in detail, are the 'best in the class'.

Companies like Xerox and Motorola have consciously set out to appraise rigorously how they manage their processes compared to companies in any industry, who are regarded as service leaders. Thus, an often quoted example is that of Xerox who in seeking to improve its order processing system found that they could learn a lot from a sports goods mail order company, L. L. Bean, who had a reputation for fast turnaround of high volume error-free orders.

The value of process benchmarking is that it enables the organization to break away from the established mould within the industry in which they compete and instead to identify best practise, wherever it may be found, with a view to incorporating it in an innovative way in their own systems. The great danger of only comparing yourself with direct competitors is the tendency to 'regression to the mean', in other words, all players in the market end up looking much the same. To outperform the competition in service, as in everything else, requires us to look outside the industry and adopt and adapt best practise from whatever source.

5 Customer service and total quality

> "How do you create a perceptible difference that sets your product above the rest? The key is service – not adequate customer service, but exemplary customer service! Extraordinary attention to the customer.
>
> "At American Express, service *is* our "differentiator" – outstanding, superior, service quality. It's part of our contract with our customers. If something goes wrong, we view it as an opportunity to demonstrate our ability to exceed our customers' expectations. We don't want our customers to be simply satisfied. We want them to be delighted!
>
> Terrence J. Smith
> Senior Vice President
> American Express Co.

There can be no doubting the revolution that has taken place in most Western companies' attitude towards quality. What was once an idea that seemed to have relevance only in the factory has now come to be recognised as the core value that has to underlie the activities of any business. This is the idea of *Total Quality*.

Total Quality Management (TQM) must extend through the entire supply chain. In other words quality has to be managed at every stage in the pipeline that connects suppliers to the business and the business to its customers. The idea is to build a 'chain of quality' such that every link in the chain is based upon a 'supplier' providing a 'customer' with total quality. In this way there will be a 'knock-on' effect which will lead to the achievement of quality service in the marketplace.

THE LINK BETWEEN SERVICE AND QUALITY

The point was made earlier in this book that customers do not buy products, they seek benefits. In so doing they evaluate competing offers in terms of the totality of product and service as well as the 'relationship' that currently exists, or potentially could exist, between themselves and the supplier and/or the brand. Customer behaviour, both at the level of individual consumers or organizational buyers, is a complex phenomenon. However we are now beginning to appreciate that service – in its widest sense – is a crucial element in this process.

The diagram below attempts to suggest how customer service can be used to gain a marketing advantage, not just by meeting customer expectations but by exceeding them. This is the concept of 'delighting the customer'. In this model the way the organization differentiates itself from its competitors is not just by the quality of the core product but by how it manages the 'service surround'. In other words we should recognize that every interaction with the customer provides an opportunity to be 'unique' and to go beyond simply meeting expectations.

Customer service and total quality

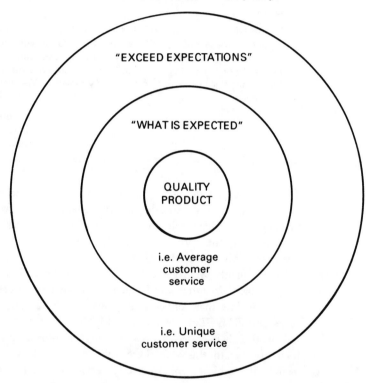

One simple way of defining service quality in this total sense is as a ratio:

$$\text{Service quality} = \frac{\text{Performance}}{\text{Expectations}}$$

Since we are able both to measure performance (as perceived by customers) and expectations (as defined by those customers) then we have a practical way of measuring service quality. Clearly any ratio less than 1 is inadequate and any ratio greater than 1 suggests that we are seen as a quality supplier. This is not to say that we should go for service 'overkill' - this is wasteful and will not enhance our position. Rather we should be seeking ways in which we can provide levels of service which are appreciated by customers and which will lead to a strengthening of the relationship.

Using the measurement techniques described in the previous sections the construction of a 'Service Barometer' as shown below can provide a powerful way of focusing management's attention upon the service quality challenge:

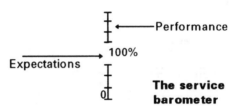

On the Service Barometer the expectations of the customer are scaled to represent 100 per cent, (in other words acceptable performance) anything beyond that represents a potential differential advantage. Conversely any performance score below the norm indicates a service quality problem.

PERFORMANCE AND EXPECTATIONS: CLOSING THE GAP

If there is a gap between service performance and expectations in the wrong direction, i.e. performance does not match expectations, what can be done about it?

The first requirement is to ensure that we fully understand what the main influences are both on expectations and upon perceptions of performance. The diagram on page 68 suggests that a number of factors contribute to the expectation of the level of service: the nature of the service/product on offer, the needs of the customer, word-of-mouth communication, past experience and corporate image. Service perceptions of performance will be influenced both by the content and the process of the service experience.

A number of researchers and commentators have sought to explain why performance and expectations may not always coincide. Essentially the view is that there are a number of potential 'service quality gaps' than can arise from the interpretations of customer expectations in the first

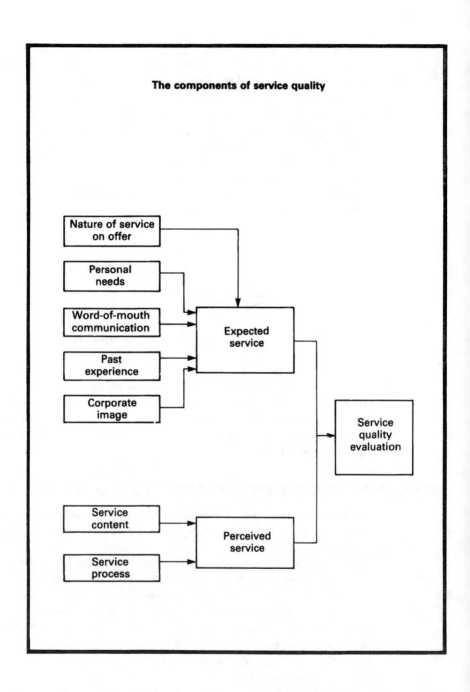

The components of service quality

place right through to service delivery failures. The model outlined in the diagram on page 69 shows how the cumulative effect of these gaps will lead to a shortfall of perceived performance against expectations:

Customer

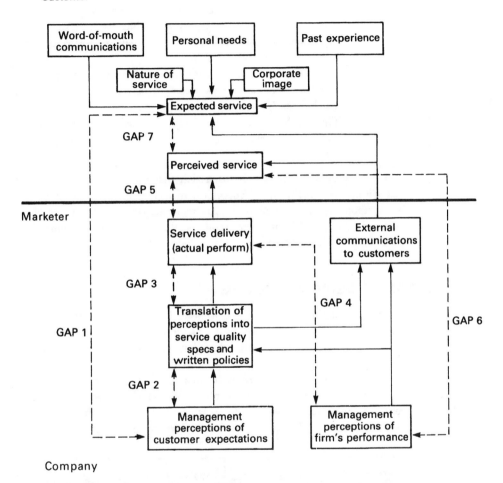

Source: Based upon Parasuraman, "A Conceptual
Model of Service Quality and its Implications
for Future Research", *Journal of Marketing* Vol 49, 1985

In summary, these gaps might be described as follows:

Gap 1   Difference between consumer expectations and management
          perceptions of consumer expectations.

Gap 2   Difference between management perceptions of consumer
          expectations and service quality specifications.

Gap 3   Difference between service quality specification and the
          service actually delivered.

Gap 4   Difference between service delivery intention and what is communicated about the service to customers.

Gap 5   Because customer perceptions are subjective and selective a gap may occur between the actual performance and customers' perceptions of it.

Gap 6   Depending upon the nature and objectivity of the feedback there may be a gap between perceived performance and management's perceptions of that performance.

Gap 7   The combined impact of Gaps 1-6 will inevitably lead to Gap 7 - the gap between expectation and perceived performance.

It will be apparent from this discussion that the key to service quality lies within the organization. Successful management of service must be based upon the idea of quality improvement across all stages in the chain outlined above. This in turn requires that the internal 'climate' is conducive to the development of a service quality culture.

THE CUSTOMER SERVICE CLIMATE

We hear a lot these days about 'Corporate Culture' and 'Shared Values'. Essentially these ideas are a reflection of the fact that organizations where everyone is moving in the same direction with the same goals in mind, are likely to be the most successful. This notion can be extended to the customer service arena in that performance is very much linked to the motivation and attitudes that people have and these are themselves a reflection of internal values. These values are in turn indicative of the customer service 'climate' that exists within the organization:

Recent research into the importance of 'corporate culture' has highlighted the direct relationship between how employees and managers feel about their own company, the values they share, the satisfaction they have in their jobs and their approach to customer service. In other words a prerequisite for becoming a service-driven company is to establish a positive internal climate which fosters positive attitudes towards customer satisfaction.

Not only is it vital that a positive customer service climate be established but it is also essential that the internal understanding of what customer service should be, matching the customer's definition and requirements, should likewise be established. Unless there is an alignment between how the customers view service (and their priorities) and how our own people view it then we have problems.

The idea of *alignment* is crucial here. We are talking about the need to bring the employee's view of service and service priorities into line with the views that the customer holds. It may also be necessary for the organization to seek a re-alignment of customer views by a programme of communications seeking to shape customer expectations. Think of it as two spotlights on a stage. At the moment, these two beams of light are some distance apart - one is the customer's viewpoint, the other the employee's - the challenge is to move the spotlights so that the beams of light coincide, that is customer service alignment.

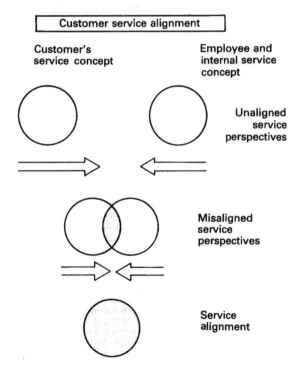

Once again the approach to adopt in seeking to achieve service alignment must be based upon objective measurement.

Research techniques of the type described in Chapter 4 should be employed to survey the internal customer service climate and to seek a measure of how employees feel about service and their view of customer priorities. A recommended approach is:

Internal customer service survey

- Flowchart the order fulfilment process.
- Identify personnel involved in order fulfilment.
- Conduct depth interviews with representative personnel to ascertain their definitions of service.
- Survey personnel to profile their ratings of customer service performance.
- Compare these ratings with actual customer ratings.
- Identify significant differences.

Secondly a survey of customers should be conducted to measure objectively their view of service priorities and performance. The next step is to compare the two and identify any areas where alignment may be necessary. The process is as shown below:

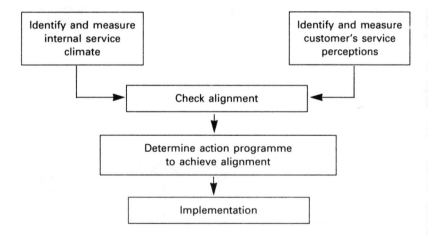

An example of the difference in how managers and customers sometimes view the world in service terms is illustrated below. In this particular case a study was carried out for a company in the office equipment market. Simultaneously service managers within the company and external customers were asked to complete a questionnaire to identify after-sales service priorities and to give an indication of how the company was performing on those service elements. The company's service managers were asked to fill in the questionnaire as they thought the customer would respond - in other words putting themselves in the customers' shoes.

As can be seen from the diagram below there were some significant differences in the external and internal views. The precise shape of the service mis-alignment was thus highlighted.

Importance score

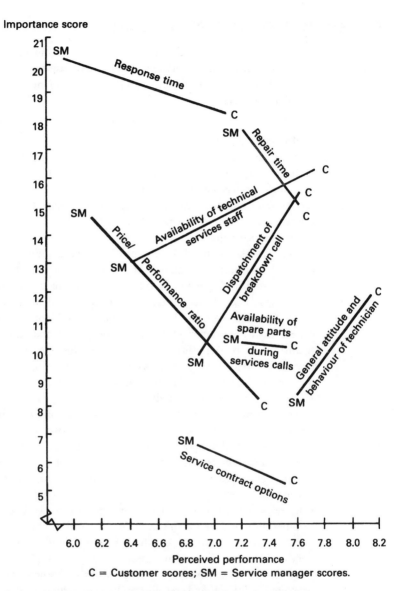

Perceived performance

C = Customer scores; SM = Service manager scores.

Source: Kasper, H., Lemmink, K. "After Sales Service Quality: Views Between Industrial Customers and Service Managers" *Industrial Marketing Management* Vol. 18, pp. 199–208, 1989

It will be seen that the service managers misjudged both the relative importance of the service elements and the performance rating that customers gave that company. What type of actions would be appropriate to overcome this misalignment?

DEVELOPING A CHANGE PROGRAMME

As we have already indicated the service alignment process can be approached from two directions. In the first case we may need to bring about an internal re-orientation and secondly we may need to re-shape customer expectations.

(i) Internal re-orientation

In most organizations there is no doubting the willingness of people to wish to satisfy customers. The problem tends to be that the systems that enable consistent service to be achieved do not exist, strategies for service tend not to be clearly defined and developed and there has been no attempt to define a service mission and hence to inculcate a set of shared service values.

The process outlined below provides some guidance on the steps involved in gaining acceptance of the service mission (see opposite).

A key step in this model is the identification of the 'do wells'. In other words what does the organization have to do well to achieve the desired ends? The definition of these 'do wells' is best done by those who are closest to the customer - the front line people and those who support them. An early step that British Airways took in their dramatic shift towards a service orientation was to empower the people, working through 'Customer First teams' (i.e. service quality circles), to identify key areas where improvement was needed and then to implement that change.

These teams ideally should be multi-functional and able to bring a broad perspective to the issues in question. Most importantly they must be given the total support of top management so that they are motivated to bring forward proposals that they know will be actioned.

It is not sufficient to do as some companies have done and appoint a Customer Service Manager and say to him or her: 'Service is now your responsibility - make it happen!' Service as we know is everyone's responsibility and hence the need for this to be reflected in the way we organize. It is questionable whether there should even be 'Customer Service Managers' in any organization.

Much can be achieved by internal workshops where the focus is upon problem definition and resolution by multi-functional teams who are empowered to institute change programmes. In other words we can learn from the Japanese who, in their search for *Kaizen*, or continuous improvement, recognize that the workforce at all levels must be involved in the search for an *implementation of* quality improvement. The success of Japanese suggestion schemes, is testament to the willingness of senior management to adopt ideas for improvement from those most closely involved. The table on page 76 compares the lack of success with suggestion schemes in the USA compared to that encountered in Japan.

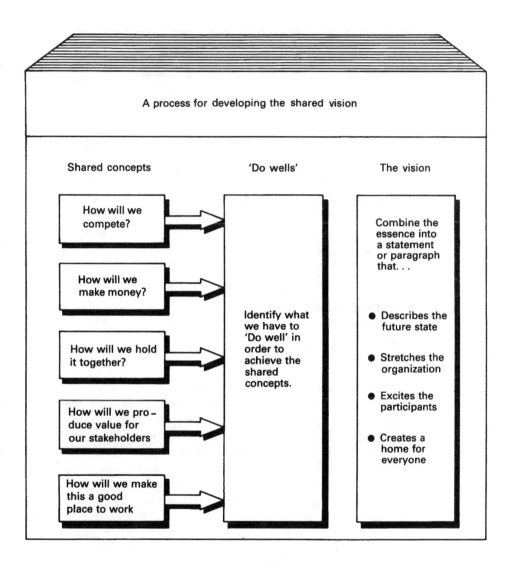

A process for developing the shared vision

Shared concepts   'Do wells'   The vision

How will we
compete?

How will we
make money?

How will we hold
it together?

How will we pro –
duce value for
our stakeholders

How will we make
this a good
place to work

Identify what
we have to
'Do well' in
order to
achieve the
shared
concepts.

Combine the
essence into
a statement
or paragraph
that. . .

● Describes the
future state

● Stretches the
organization

● Excites the
participants

● Creates a
home for
everyone

Source: Norton, D.P., "Breaking Functional Gridlock: The Case for a Mission-Oriented Organization". *Stage by Stage* Vol. 8 No. 2, 1988, Norton & Co, Lexington, Mass. USA

	USA	Japan
Number of eligible	8,364,865	1,685,412
Total suggestions received	1,010,889	52,989,345
Number of suggestions per 100 eligible	13	3,145
Number of employees submitting per 100 eligible	9	80
Adoption rate	29.0%	82.5%
Average award payments per adoption	$545.68	$2.7
Average net savings per adoption	$7,663	$43
Net savings per 100 eligible employees	$26,870	$356,531

(ii) Re-shaping customer expectations

So many perceived service quality failures arise because customer expectation differed from the planned offer from the supplier. In other words the customer expected X and all along we planned to offer Y. This problem would obviously be avoided if the supplier clearly defined and communicated the service offer. Ultimately this comes down to the quality of communications between the organization and its customers. It is often the case that customer communications are not managed on a *pro-active* basis but rather on a *re-active* basis. What this means is that the supplier will tend to respond to stimuli from the customer, e.g. queries, orders, complaints, rather than to have a managed customer communications programme. For example, in the managed communications environment, the customer would never have to enquire about the status of an order - the supplier would keep the customer informed on its progress at all stages. Likewise there would be no 'surprises' for the customer, e.g. non-availability of stock would be immediately communicated, lead-times would be transparent and overall the customer would know exactly what to expect. Bearing in mind that a crucial part of the service management process is the meeting of customer expectations it will be understood that communications play a major role in the establishment of those expectations in the first place. There are a variety of ways in which a customer communication system may be established ranging from telephone 'hot lines' to electronic data interchange. In practice it is not so much a single channel of communication but a number, all of which are managed and pro-active. The diagram below identifies some of the most effective ways of developing close and continuous communication linkages with the customer base and these are described below:

Customer service communication process

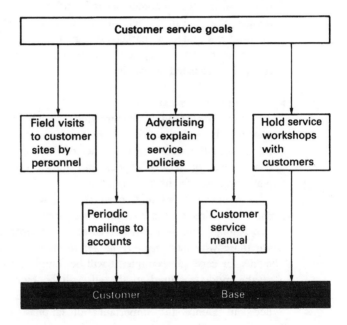

● *Field visits to customer sites by personnel*
  This can be a very effective means of both communicating with customers and improving internal motivation. The idea is that our internal people who normally never see customers and often only know them as company names or account numbers, should visit customers from time to time. The effect can be even more powerful when personnel visit their 'opposite numbers'. So for instance people who are responsible for preparing invoices could visit the accounts department of the customer and meet those who have to process the invoice once received. Similarly people from the warehouse responsible for assembling and packing orders could visit those responsible at the customer's premises for receiving goods. As

well as good customer relations, there will be frequent occasions where ideas for improvement in specific areas can be sparked off through these meetings.

● *Periodic mailing to customer accounts*
These can take many forms but perhaps the most effective are customer service newsletters which are informative and report on changes in procedures or improvements in the service field. These need not be produced too often and should always be informative - the last thing the customer needs is still more 'junk mail'. On a more regular basis it can be helpful to the customer to receive fact sheets on products and end markets and an idea well worth considering is a customer service 'update' on availability and delivery which is regularly circulated to customers.

● *Advertising to explain service policies*
An observable trend is the growing use by service-oriented companies of advertising to emphasize their service offer. Not only does this inform the would-be Customer of the service package and establish a level of service expectations but it can also be a powerful marketing tool in its own right.

It is not just potential customers to whom these advertisements should be directed but also *existing* customers. Research has indicated that amongst the people who read advertisements in the greatest detail are those who have *recently bought the product*. Thus with advertisements for cars, for example, it will be found that the recent purchaser of the model featured in the ad. will be highly likely to read it - primarily to seek reassurance that he or she has made the right decision! Hence the importance of emphasizing the desire for a relationship through service in such communications.

● *Develop a customer service manual*
We have several times emphasized the importance of managing the customers' expectations of service and one effective contribution to this process can be through the means of a customer service manual.

A customer service manual might take many forms but essentially it is a document given to customers that defines the organization's customer service goals and details the procedures whereby business is transacted between the parties. Hence the manual would begin with quantified service objectives in terms of delivery lead-times, stock availability and so on, it would provide specimen copies of basic documents such as delivery notes, invoices, bills of lading etc. It would list key executives' names and telephone numbers (including home numbers) and provide details of 'hot line' services and order status enquiry systems. In fact every aspect of the formal relationship that is sought between the organization and its customers should be included in the manual.

The result can be a document of tremendous practical value as well as contributing to the customer's perception of the business as a service-oriented company.

- *Hold workshops with customers*

  There are many areas of mutual concern between buyers and suppliers and consequently there will be advantages in bringing teams together from both parties on a regular basis. These meetings are not confrontations but problem-solving workshops which seek to improve the quality of service provided.

  Rather like the customer visits proposed earlier, much can be gained by bringing together, say, the commercial and accounts people in the supplying company with those responsible in the buying company for dealing with invoices and supplier originated documentation.

  In companies selling direct to end users, e.g. a retailer or a service provider like a bank or airline, such meetings might take the form of feedback sessions and customer service 'focus' groups where new opportunities for service enhancement are sought.

These are just a few of the ways in which the organization can develop continuing and open channels of communication with its customers, the objective of this customer communication programme being to ensure that in every transaction customers knows exactly what they can expect.

THE INTERNAL CUSTOMER

Many companies who have set out to develop service quality improvement programmes as part of their Total Quality Management effort have found it advantageous to adopt the idea of the 'Internal Customer'. Basically the philosophy that underlies the notion of the internal customer is that everyone in the organization must 'serve' someone. Behind this fairly obvious statement is the radical notion that anyone who works for an organization must know who their customer is and be fully aware of the service needs of that customer. In this way a 'chain' of customer service is established which will ensure that the entire organization is focused upon the single goal of customer satisfaction.

Rank Xerox were an early pioneer of this concept and they have extended it to the point where all bonuses for their senior executives are linked to an index of customer satisfaction (see box on page 80). So even though a manager may not have direct end-customer contact, they are all intimately aware of the impact of superior customer service. Perhaps this is the ultimate example of 'putting your money where your mouth is'!

An incentive scheme worth copying

By Derek Harris, Industrial Editor

Rank Xerox, the copiers and office systems company, has completed its first year with what it believes is a unique incentive payments scheme for senior executives linked to customer satisfaction – and the executives, in most of Europe, have come out of it on the winning side.

They are receiving on average a 2.5 per cent salary increase over and above the 6 per cent salary rise already being paid.

At the same time Rank Xerox reported turnover up 4 per cent but with an underlying profits growth of 23 per cent. Rank Xerox is 51 per cent owned by Xerox Corporation and 49 per cent by the Rank Organisation.

The incentive scheme will have cost between £100,000 and £200,000 according to Mr Roland Magnin, managing director and chief executive of Rank Xerox and creator of the scheme. The exact cost is still being worked out because it applied throughout the company's European operations involving 135

senior executives – the payout has varied in each national operation according to the results achieved.

The British operation had satisfaction levels at about the point which yielded the 2.5 per cent average salary boost, said Mr Magnin. One country earned no salary boost – and Mr Magnin will not benefit from the scheme. "It would not be appropriate for me to benefit."

Mr Magnin is sanguine about the scheme's cost because customer satisfaction was 4 percentage points high than in the previous year. The targets on customer satisfaction and loyalty had been 85 per cent, with loyalty demonstrated by a customer retaining a Rank Xerox product throughout the year. At the year-end, 89 per cent of customers were satisfied and the customer loyalty level stood at 88 per cent.

The scheme this year has a greater weighting for customer loyalty – the "most realistic" test of customer satisfaction. It is being extended, in the form of an incentive bonus, to all staff at the Rank Xerox international headquarters

at Marlow, Buckinghamshire, and at other European operating companies.

This year will keep the senior executive on their toes because a slip in customer satisfaction would lose them the appropriate percentage of the planned annual salary rise. But losses or gains are limited by imposing a 4 percentage points maximum movement up or down.

THE TIMES
February 10 1989

LEADERSHIP THROUGH SERVICE QUALITY

We began the discussion in Chapter 1 by highlighting the need for a concerted effort to seek competitive advantage through customer service.

This is a message that has now gained widespread acceptance even though actual progress may have been slow. To paraphrase one of the gurus of quality: "service quality is a journey not a destination". The meaning behind this slogan is profound - there is a goal, but the closer we get to it the harder we have to strive.

We now have standards for quality which can be seen as targets. In the UK it is BS 5750, a standard laid down by the British Standards Institute (see Appendix 3). Internationally the equivalent standard is IS 9000, determined by the International Standards Organisation. These standards provide a benchmark against which customers and potential customers can judge the service offer. Worthy though these schemes are, the real challenge to those companies seeking leadership in their markets is to go beyond the industry norm to truly 'delight the customer'.

One of the most significant developments in North America in this context was the creation by Congress in 1987 of the Malcolm Baldrige National Quality Award. The award was established to recognize US companies that excel in quality achievement and quality management. In the few years of its existence it has come to be recognized as one of the most comprehensive attempts to benchmark a company's progress towards quality and service excellence. Whilst it is primarily intended as a competitive award it has become accepted as the best definition of total quality criteria for any organisation seeking to improve its performance in the service and quality arena.

The award is based upon a number of basic concepts:

- Quality is defined by the customer.

- The senior leadership of businesses needs to create clear quality values and build the values into the way the company operates.

- Quality excellence derives from well-designed and well-executed systems and processes.

- Continuous improvement must be part of the management of all systems and processes.

- Companies need to develop goals, as well as strategic and operational plans to achieve quality leadership.

- Shortening the response time of all operations and processes of the company needs to be part of the quality improvement effort.

- Operations and decisions of the company need to be based upon facts and data.

- All employees must be suitably trained and developed and involved in quality activities.

- Design quality and defect and error prevention should be major elements of the quality system.

- Companies need to communicate quality requirements to suppliers and work to elevate supplier quality performance.

Many companies have now adopted the criteria of the Malcolm Baldrige Award as the basis for their own service quality improvement programmes. These criteria are detailed in Appendix 2 and are worthy of close examination by any organization that seeks to achieve competitive advantage through service and quality differentiation.

It is no coincidence that the 1989 award winner was Xerox who have successfully used the twin strategies of service and quality to halt the erosion of their once dominant world market share in the plain paper copying business. Quite justifiably, they now use the honour of the award as one of the bases for their marketing communications (see the box on page 82).

XEROX

If you can stand the pain, look at your company through the eyes of your customers.

We would like to express our pride and gratitude for having won the Baldrige Award. We'd also like to share with you some of the basic principles we discovered in our quest for quality.

1. You have to look at your company through the eyes of your customers—even if it hurts. You have to let them define quality for you.

2. You have to have commitment from the top down, from the CEO to the mailroom.

3. You have to establish benchmarks that really stretch you. Set impossible goals. Then meet them.

4. You must get your suppliers involved. In 1983, when we began our Leadership Through Quality process, 92% of parts received from suppliers were defect-free, a fair standard for the industry. Today we have attained 99.97% defect-free parts.

Our government has made quality a national imperative. In 1987 Congress created the Malcolm Baldrige National Quality Award. One financial

---

Categories covered in the application for the Malcolm Baldrige Quality Award.

1. Leadership. How has senior management contributed to the quality process?

2. Information and Analysis. How effective is your collecting and analyzing information leading to quality?

3. Planning. How have you integrated quality into your business plans?

4. Human Resource Utilization. What have you done to involve all employees? How have you informed them? Motivated them?

5. Quality Assurances. This focuses on the process put in place for sustaining quality.

6. Quality Assurance Results. The one category that actually looks at your products and services.

7. Customer Satisfaction. How do your customers like your products? How do you know they do?

---

journalist has called it "a national treasure." Another writes, "It takes plenty of work to capture the new national Holy Grail of quality. Happily, companies that lose get nearly as much benefit as the victors." (Jeremy Main, *Fortune*, April 23, 1990)

It is tough. We underwent a grueling scrutiny—some 400 hours of analyses and on-site inspections by the Baldrige examiners. What they're interested in is the process. But

---

if you apply for it, you can't lose. It will expose your strengths and weaknesses unsparingly. And, if you're serious, it will provide a focus that will send a shiver of energy through the spine of your company.

Since quality became the driving force of our company, our copy quality has set the standard in the industry, and our 1090 copier has been named the best in the world. We have stemmed the loss of market share to foreign competition. We have increased the satisfaction of our customers. We have also increased our number of customers.

Xerox is committed to sustaining the quality process we have entered into. Above all, we have learned that in the race for quality, there is no finish line.

To find out more about the Xerox Quality Process and the Malcolm Baldrige National Quality Award, please write to: Xerox Corporation, P.O. Box 24, Rochester, NY 14692. Or call: 1-800-TEAM-XRX, Ext. 327A.

**XEROX
The Document Company**

© 1990 XEROX CORPORATION XEROX® is a trademark of XEROX CORPORATION

However it is not just the big name, global companies who are discovering that service quality reaps dividends. Many smaller companies have established loyal and growing customer bases through their attention to customer satisfaction. What we can learn from these successes, whether the company be large or small, international or local, is that there are a number of simple, yet powerful, prescriptions for success in the service arena. Two of the leading commentators on service-based marketing strategies, Albrecht and Zemke, have listed nine characteristics of success below:

Characteristics of successful service-oriented companies

1. They have a strong vision – a strategy for service that is clearly developed and clearly communicated.

2. They practise visible management.

3. They "talk" service routinely.

4. They have customer-friendly service systems.

5. They balance, high-tech with high-touch, that is, they temper their systems and methods with the personal factor.

6. They recruit, hire, train, and promote for service.

7. They market service to their customers.

8. They market service internally, that is, to their employees.

9. They measure service and make the results available to the service people.

Source: Karl Albrecht & Ron Zemke
Service America' Dow-Jones Irwin 1985

To this list we might add a tenth prescription:

> "Successful service-oriented companies plan, control and monitor their service programmes and seek to improve continuously their service performance."

Appendix 1 Customer service audit checklist

The theme throughout *The Customer Service Planner* has been the need to monitor and measure performance against customer requirements. To aid in this process the following checklist is provided, highlighting the key issues and questions to be included in a Customer Service Audit:

- Do you have a written customer service policy?
- Is this given a wide circulation within the company?
- Do customers receive a copy of this policy?
- Is customer service included in the marketing plan?
- What elements of customer service do you regularly monitor?
- Do you monitor competitive service performance?
- Do you know the true costs of providing customer service?
- Do customers have direct access to information on stock availability and delivery?
- How do you report to customers on order status?
- Is there a single point of contact for customers in your company?
- Is any attempt made to estimate the cost of customer service failures (e.g. a part delivery, late delivery, etc.)?
- Do you seek to measure the costs of providing different levels of service?
- Do you have internal service measures as well as external measures?
- How do you communicate service policies to customers?
- What is your average order cycle time?
- Do you monitor actual order-to-delivery lead-time performance?
- Do you have a system for accounting for customer profitability?
- Does the Chief Executive regularly receive a report on customer service performance?
- Do you consciously seek to hire individuals with a positive attitude towards customer service?
- Do you use quality control concepts in managing customer service?
- Do you differentiate service levels by product?
- Do you differentiate customer service levels by customer type?
- Do you have a standard cost for a stock-out (e.g. cost of lost sales, cost of back orders etc.)?
- Do you provide customers with a customer service manual?
- Do you monitor the internal customer service 'climate' on a regular basis?

- Does your customer service organization effectively manage the client relationship from order to delivery and beyond?
- How do you monitor and respond to complaints?
- How responsive are you to claims from customers?

Appendix 2　Malcolm Baldrige award criteria

1991 EXAMINATION CATEGORIES AND ITEMS
Malcolm Baldrige National Quality Award

1991 EXAMINATION

1.0 LEADERSHIP (100pts.)

The *Leadership* category examines how senior executives create and sustain clear and visible quality values along with a management system to guide all activities of the company toward quality excellence. Also examined are the senior executives' and the company's quality leadership in the external community and how the company integrates its public responsibilities with its quality values and practices.

1.1 Senior Executive Leadership *(40pts.)*
Describe the senior executives' leadership, personal involvement, and visibility in developing and maintaining an environment for quality excellence.

Areas to address
a. senior executives' leadership, personal involvement, and visibility in quality-related activities of the company: (1) goal setting; (2) planning; (3) reviewing company quality performance; (4) communicating with employees: and (5) recognizing employee contributions. Other activities may include participating in teams, learning about the quality of domestic and international competitors, and meeting with customers and suppliers.
b. senior executives' approach to building quality values into the leadership process of the company.
c. senior executives' leadership and communication of quality excellence to groups outside the company. Groups may include national, state, community, trade, business, professional, education, health care, standards, and government organizations.

Notes:
(1) The term 'senior executives' refers to the highest-training official of the organization applying for the Award and those reporting directly to that official.
(2) The type and extent of the activities of senior executives within and outside the company could depend upon company size, resources, and other business factors.

1.2 Quality Values *(15 pts.)*
Describe the company's quality values, how they are projected in a consistent manner, and how adoption of the values throughout the company is determined and reinforced.

Areas to address
a. brief summary of the content of policy, mission, or guidelines that demonstrate the company's quality values.
b. company's communications activities to project the quality values throughout the company. Briefly describe what is communicated and the means and frequency of communications.
c. how the company determines and evaluates how well the quality values have been adopted throughout the company, such as through surveys, interviews, or other means, and how employee adoption is reinforced.

1.3 Management for Quality *(25 pts.)*
Describe how the quality values are integrated into day-to-day leadership, management, and supervision of all company units.

Areas to address
a. key approaches for involving, and encouraging leadership in, all levels of management and supervision in quality; principal roles and responsibilities at each level.
b. key approaches for promoting cooperation among managers and supervisors across different levels and different functions of the company.
c. types, frequency, and content of reviews of company and of unit quality performance; types of actions taken to assist units not performing according to plans or goals.
d. key indicators the company uses to evaluate the effectiveness of its approaches to integrating quality values into day-to-day management and how the evaluation is used to improve its approaches.

Note:
Key indicators refer to principal measures of some characteristics of quality or effectiveness.

1.4 Public Responsibility *(20 pts.)*
Describe how the company extends its quality leadership to the external community and includes its responsibilities to the public for health, safety, environmental protection, and ethical business practice in its quality policies and improvement activities.

Areas to address
a. how the company promotes quality awareness and sharing with external groups. Groups may include national, state, community, trade, business, professional, education, health care, standards, and government organizations.

b. how the company encourages employee leadership and involvement in quality activities of organizations mentioned above.

c. how the company includes its public responsibilities such as business ethics, public health and safety, environmental protection, and waste management into its quality policies and practices. For each area relevant and important to the company's business, briefly summarize: (1) principal quality improvement goals and how they are set: (2) principal improvement methods: (3) principal indicators used to monitor quality and (4) how and how often progress is reviewed.

Note:

(1) Health and safety of employees are not covered in this item. These are addressed in item 4.5.

2.0 INFORMATION AND ANALYSIS (70 pts.)

The *Information and Analysis* category examines the scope, validity, use, and management of data and information that underlie the company's overall quality management system. Also examined is the adequacy of the data, information, and analysis to support a responsive, prevention-based approach to quality and customer satisfaction built upon 'management by fact.'

2.1 Scope and Management of Quality Data and Information *(20 pts.)*
Describe the company's base of data and information used for planning, day-to-day management, and evaluation of quality, and how data and information reliability, timeliness, and access are assured.

Areas to address

a. (1) criteria for selecting data to be included in the quality-related data and information base; and (2) scope and types of data: customer-related; internal operations and processes; employee-related; safety, health, and regulatory; quality performance; supplier quality; and other.

b. processes and techniques the company uses to ensure reliability, consistency, standardization, review, timely update, and rapid access throughout the company. If applicable, describe approach to ensuring software quality.

c. how the company evaluates and improves the scope and quality of its data and information and how it shortens the cycle from data gathering to access.

Note:

(1) The purpose of this item is to permit the applicant to demonstrate

the *breadth and depth* of the data assembled as part of its total quality management system. Applicants should give brief descriptions of the types of data under major headings such as 'employees' and subheadings such as 'education and training,' 'teams,' and 'recognition.' Under each subheading, give a brief description of the data and information. Actual data should not be reported in this item. Such data are requested in other examination items.

(2) Information on the scope and management of competitive and benchmark data is requested in item 2.2.

2.2 Competitive Comparisons and Benchmarks *(30pts.)*

Describe the company's approach to selecting quality related competitive comparisons and world-class benchmarks to support quality planning, evaluation, and improvement.

Areas to address

a. criteria and rationale the company uses for seeking competitive comparisons and benchmarks: (1) relationship to company goals and priorities for improvement of product and service quality and/or company operations; (2) with whom to compare – within and outside the company's industry.

b. current scope of competitive and benchmark data: (1) product and service quality; (2) customer satisfaction and other customer data; (3) supplier performance; (4) employee data; (5) internal operations, business processes, and support services; and (6) other. For each type: (a) list sources of comparisons and benchmarks, including company and independent testing or evaluation; and (b) how each type of data is used.

c. how the company evaluates and improves the scope, sources, and uses of competitive and benchmark data.

2.3 Analysis of Quality Data and Information *(20 pts.)*

Describe how data and information are analyzed to support the company's overall quality objectives.

Areas to address

a. how data described in 2.1 and 2.2, separately and in combination, are analyzed to support: (1) company planning and priorities; (2) company-level review of quality performance; (3) improvement of internal operations, business processes, and support services; (4) determination of product and service features and levels of quality performance that best predict improvement in customer satisfaction; and (5) quality improvement projections based upon potential use of alternative strategies or technologies.

b. how the company evaluates and improves its analytical capabilities and shortens the cycle of analysis and access to analytical results.

Note:

This item focuses primarily on analysis for company-level evaluation and decision making. Some other items request information based on analysis of specific sets of data for special purposes such as human resource practices and complaint management.

3.0 STRATEGIC QUALITY PLANNING PROCESS (60 pts.)

The *Strategic Quality Planning* category examines the company's planning process for achieving or retaining quality leadership and how the company integrates quality improvement planning into overall business planning. Also examined are the company's short-term and longer-term plans to achieve and/or sustain a quality leadership position.

3.1 Strategic Quality Planning Process *(35 pts.)*

Describe the company's strategic quality planning process for short-term 1–2 years) and longer-term (3 years or more) quality leadership and customer satisfaction.

Areas to address

a. how goals for quality leadership are set using: (1) current and future quality requirements for leadership in the company's target markets; and (2) company's current quality levels and trends versus competitors' in these markets.

b. principal types of data, information, and analysis used in developing plans and evaluating feasibility based upon goals: (1) customer requirements; (2) process capabilities; (3) competitive and benchmark data; and (4) supplier capabilities; outline how these data are used in developing plans.

c. how strategic pans and goals are implemented and reviewed: (1) how specific plans, goals, and performance indicators are deployed to all work units and suppliers; and (2) how resources are committed for key requirements such as capital expenditures and training; and (3) how performance relative to plans and goals is reviewed and acted upon.

d. how the goal-setting and strategic planning processes are evaluated and improved.

Notes:

(1) Strategic quality plans address in detail how the company will pursue market leadership through providing superior quality products and services and through improving the effectiveness of all operations of the company.

(2) Item 3.1 focuses on the processes of goal setting and strategic planning. Item 3.2 focuses on actual goals and plans.

3.2 Quality Goals and Plans *(25 pts.)*

Summarize the company's goals and strategies. Outline principal quality plans for the short term (1,2 years) and longer term (3 years or more).

Areas to address

a. major quality goals and principal strategies for achieving these goals.

b. principal short-term plans: (1) summary of key requirements and performance indicators deployed to work units and suppliers; and (2) resources committed to accomplish the key requirements.

c. principal longer-term plans: brief summary of major requirements, and how they will be met.

d. two- to five-year projection of significant changes in the company's most important quality levels. Describe how these levels may be expected to compare with those of key competitors over this time period.

Note:

The company's most important quality levels are those for the key product and service quality features. Projections are estimates of future quality levels based upon implementation of the plans described in item 3.2.

4.0 HUMAN RESOURCE UTILIZATION (150 pts.)

The *Human Resource Utilization* category examines the effectiveness of the company's efforts to develop and realize the full potential of the work force, including management, and to maintain an environment conducive to full participation, quality leadership, and personal and organizational growth.

4.1 Human Resource Management *(20pts.)*

Describe how the company's overall human resource management effort supports its quality objectives.

Areas to address

a. how human resource plans are derived from the quality goals, strategies, and plans outlined in 3.2: (1) short term (1-2 years); and (2) longer term (3 years or more). Address major specific requirements such as training, development, hiring, involvement, empowerment, and recognition.

b. key quality goals and improvement methods for human resource management practices such as hiring and career development.

c. how the company analyzes and uses its overall employee-related data to evaluate and improve the effectiveness of all categories and all types of employees.

Notes:

(1) Human resource plans and improvement activities might include one or more of the following: mechanisms for promoting cooperation such as internal customer/supplier techniques or other internal partnerships; initiatives to promote labour-management cooperation such as partnerships with unions; creation or modifications in recognition systems; mechanisms for increasing or broadening employee responsibilities; and education and training initiatives They might also include developing partnerships with educational institutions to develop employees and to help ensure the future supply of well-prepared employees.

(2) 'Types of employees' takes into account factors such as employment status, bargaining unit membership, and demographic makeup.

4.2 Employee Involvement *(40 pts.)*

Describe the means available for all employees to contribute effectively to meeting the company's quality objectives; summarize trends and current levels of involvement.

Areas to address

a. management practices and specific mechanisms, such as teams or suggestion systems, the company uses to promote employee contributions to quality objectives, individually and in groups. Summarize how and when the company gives feedback.

b. company actions to increase employee authority to act (empowerment), responsibility, and innovation. Summarize principal goals for all categories of employees.

c. key indicators the company uses to evaluate the extent and effectiveness of involvement by all categories and types of employees and how the indicators are used to improve employee involvement.

d. trends and current levels of involvement by all categories of employees. Use the most important indicator(s) of effective employee involvement for each category of employee.

Note:

Different involvement goals and indicators may be set for different categories of employees, depending upon company needs and upon the types of responsibilities of each employee category.

4.3 Quality Education and Training (40 pts.)

Describe how the company decides what quality education and training is needed by employees and how it utilizes the knowledge and skills acquired; summarize the types of quality education and training received by employees in all employee categories.

Areas to address

a. (1) how the company assesses needs for the types and amounts of quality education and training received by all categories of employees. (Describe how the needs assessment addresses work unit requirements to include or have access to skills in problem analysis and problem solving to meet their quality objectives.) (2) methods for the delivery of quality education and training; and (3) how the company ensures on-the-job reinforcement of knowledge and skills.

b. summary and trends in quality education and training received by employees. The summary and trends should address: (1) quality orientation of new employees; (2) per cent of employees receiving quality education and training in each employee category annually; (3) average hours of quality education and training annually per employee; (4) per cent of employees who have received quality education and training; and (5) per cent of employees who have received education and training in statistical and other quantitative problem-solving methods.

c. key methods and indicators the company uses to evaluate and improve the effectiveness of its quality education and training. Describe how the indicators are used to improve the quality education and training of all categories and types of employees.

Note:

Quality education and training addresses the knowledge and skills employees need to meet the quality objectives associated with their responsibilities. This may include basic quality awareness, problem solving, meeting customer requirements, and other quality-related aspects of skills.

4.4 Employee Recognition and Performance Measurement *(25 pts.)*

Describe how the company's recognition and performance measurement processes support quality objectives; summarize trends in recognition.

Areas to address

a. how recognition, reward, and performance measurement for individuals and groups, including managers, supports the company's quality objectives; (1) how quality relative to other business considerations such as schedules and financial results is reinforced; and (2) how employees are involved in the development and improvement of performance measurements.

b. trends in recognition and reward of individuals and groups, by employee category, for contributions to quality.

c. key indicators the company uses to evaluate and improve its recognition, reward, and performance measurement processes.

4.5 Employee Well-Being and Morale *(25 pts.)*

Describe how the company maintains a work environment conducive to the well-being and growth of all employees; summarize trends and levels in key indicators of well-being and morale.

Areas to address

a. how well-being and morale factors such as health, safety, satisfaction, and ergonomics are included in quality improvement activities. Summarize principal improvement goals and methods for each factor relevant and important to the company's work environment. For accidents and work-related health problems, describe how underlying causes are determined and how adverse conditions are prevented.

b. mobility, flexibility, and retraining in job assignments to support employee development and/or to accommodate changes in technology, improved productivity, or changes in work processes.

c. special services, facilities and opportunities the company makes available to employees. These might include one or more of the following: counselling, assistance, recreational or cultural, and non-work-related education.

d. how employee satisfaction is determined and interpreted for use in quality improvement.

e. trends and levels in key indicators of well-being and morale such as safety, absenteeism, turnover, attrition rate for customer-contact personnel, satisfaction, grievances, strikes, and worker compensation. Explain important adverse results, if any, and how problems were resolved or current status. Compare the current levels of the most significant indicators with those of industry averages and industry leaders.

5.0 QUALITY ASSURANCE OF PRODUCTS AND SERVICES (140 pts.)

The *Quality Assurance of Products and Services* category examines the systematic approaches used by the company for assuring quality of goods and services based primarily upon process design and control, including control of procured materials, parts, and services. Also examined is the integration of process control with continuous quality improvement.

5.1 Design and Introduction of Quality Products and Services *(35 pts.)*

Describe how new and/or improved products and services are designed and introduced and how processes arc designed to meet key product and service quality requirements.

Areas to address

a. how designs of products, services, and processes are developed so that: (1) customer requirements are translated into design requirements; (2) all quality requirements are addressed early in the overall design process by all appropriate company units; (3) designs are coordinated and integrated to include all phases of production and delivery; and (4) a process control plan is developed that involves selecting and setting key process characteristics for production and delivery of products and services and how these characteristics are to be measured and controlled.

b. how designs are reviewed and validated taking into account key factors: (1) product and service performance; (2) process capability and future requirements; and (3) supplier capability and future requirements.

c. how the company evaluates and improves the effectiveness of its designs and design processes and how it shortens the design-to-introduction cycle.

Notes:

(1) Design and introduction may include modification and variants of existing products and services and/or new products and services emerging from research and development.

(2) Service and manufacturing businesses should interpret product and service requirements to include all product- and service-related requirements at all stages of production, delivery, and use. See also Item 7.1, Note (3).

(3) Depending on their type of business, applicants need to consider many factors in product and service design such as heath, safety, long-term performance, measurement capability, process capability, maintainability, and supplier capability. Applicant responses should reflect the key requirements of the products and services they deliver.

5.2 Process Quality Control *(20 pts.)*

Describe how the processes used to produce the company's products and services are controlled.

Areas to address

a. how the company assures that processes are controlled within limits set in process design. Include information on: (1) types and frequencies of measurements; and (2) what is measured, such as process, product, and service characteristics.

b. for out-of-control occurrences, describe: (1) how root causes are determined; (2) how corrections are made so that future occurrences are prevented; and (3) how corrections are verified.

c. how the company evaluates the quality of the measurements used in process quality control and assures measurement quality control.

Notes:

(1) For manufacturing and service companies with measurement? requirements, it is necessary to demonstrate that measurement accuracy and precision meet process, service, and product requirements (measurement quality assurance). For physical, chemical, and engineering measurements, indicate approaches for ensuring that measurements are traceable to national standards through calibrations, reference materials, or other means.

(2) Verification of corrections and verification of improvements in 5.2b, 5.3c, and 5.4b should include comparison with expected or predicted results.

5.3 Continuous Improvement of Processes *(20pts.)*
Describe how processes used to produce products and services are continuously improved.

Areas to address

a. principal types of data and information the company uses to determine needs and opportunities for improvement in processes: (1) data from day-to-day process control; (2) field data such as customer data, data on product and service performance, and data on competitors' performance; (3) evaluation of all process steps; (4) process benchmark data; and (5) data of other types such as from process research and development and evaluation of new technology or alternative processes.

b. how the company evaluates potential changes in processes to select from among alternatives.

c. how the company integrates process improvement with day-to-day process quality control: (1) resetting process characteristics; (2) verification of improvements; and (3) ensuring effective use by all appropriate company units.

Note:
The focus of this item is on *improvement* of the primary processes used to produce the company's products and services, not on maintaining them or on correcting out-of-control occurrences, which is the focus of Item 5.2.

5.4 Quality Assessment *(15pts.)*
Describe how the company assesses the quality of its systems, processes, practices, products, and services.

Areas to address

a. approaches the company uses to assess the quality of its systems, processes, practices, products, and services such as process reviews or audits. Include the types and frequencies of assessments, what is assessed, who conducts the assessments, and how the validity of assessment tools is assured.

b. how assessment findings are used to improve systems, processes, practices, training, or supplier requirements. Include how the company verifies that improvements are effective.

5.5 Documentation *(10pts.)*

Describe documentation and other modes of knowledge preservation and knowledge transfer to support quality assurance, quality assessment, and quality improvement.

Areas to address

a. (1) principal quality-related purposes of documents such as for recording procedures and practices and for retaining key records; and (2) uses of documents such as in standardization, orientation of new employees, training, maintaining records for legal purposes, or for quality-related tracking of products, processes, and services.

b. how the company improves its documentation system: (1) to simplify and harmonize documents; (2) to keep pace with changes in practice, technology, and systems; (3) to ensure rapid access wherever needed; and (4) to dispose of obsolete documents.

Note:
Documents may be written or computerized.

5.6 Business Process and Support Service Quality *(20pts.)*

Summarize process quality, quality assessment, and quality improvement activities for business processes and support services.

Areas to address

a. summary of process quality control and quality assessment activities for key business processes and support services: (1) how principal process quality requirements are set using customer requirements or the requirements of other company units served ('internal customers'); (2) how and how often process quality is measured; and (3) types and frequencies of quality assessments and who conducts them.

b. summary of quality improvement activities for key business processes and support services: (1) principal quality improvement goals and how they are set; (2) principal process evaluation and improvement activities, including how processes are simplified and response time shortened; (3) principal indicators used to measure quality; and (4) how and how often progress is reviewed

Notes:
(1) Business processes and support services might include activities and operations involving finance and accounting software services, sales, marketing, information services, purchasing, personnel legal services, plant and facilities management, research and development, and secretarial and other administrative services.
(2) The purpose of this item is to permit applicants to highlight separately the quality assurance, quality assessment, and quality improvement activities for functions that support the primary processes through which products and services are produced and delivered. Together, Items 5.1, 5.2, 5.3, 5.4, 5.5, 5.6, and 5.7 should cover all operations, processes, and activities of all work units. However, the selection of support services and business processes for inclusion in Item 5.6 depends on the type of business and quality system and should be made by the applicant.

5.7 Supplier Quality *(20pts.)*
Describe how the quality of materials, components, and services furnished by other businesses is assured, assessed, and improved.

Areas to address
a. approaches used to define and communicate the company's specific quality requirements to suppliers. Include: (1) the principal quality requirements for the company's most important suppliers; and (2) the principal quality indicators the company uses to communicate and monitor supplier quality.
b. methods used to assure that the company's quality requirements are met by suppliers. Methods may include audits, process reviews, receiving inspection, certification, and testing.
c. strategy and current actions to improve the quality and responsiveness of suppliers. These may include partnerships, training, incentives and recognition, and supplier selection.

Note:
The term 'supplier' as used here refers to other company providers of goods and services. The use of these goods and services may occur at any stage in the production, delivery, and use of the company's products and services. Thus, suppliers include businesses such as distributors, dealers, and franchises as well as those that provide materials and components.

6.0 QUALITY RESULTS (180 pts.)

The *Quality Results* category examines quality levels and quality improvement based upon objective measures derived from analysis of customer requirements and expectations and from analysis of business operations. Also examined are current quality levels in relation to those of competing firms.

6.1 Product and Service Quality Results *(90pts.)*

Summarize trends in quality improvement and current quality levels for key product and service features; compare the company's current quality levels with those of competitors and world leaders.

Areas to address
a. trends and current levels for all key measures of product and service quality.
b. current quality level comparisons with principal competitors in the company's key markets, industry averages, industry leaders, and world leaders. Briefly explain bases for comparison such as: (1) independent surveys, studies, or laboratory testing; (2) benchmarks; and (3) company evaluations and testing. Describe how objectivity and validity of comparisons are assured.

Notes:
(1) Key product and service measures are measures relative to the set of all important features of the company's products and services. These measures, taken together, best represent the *most important factors that predict customer satisfaction and quality in customer use.* Examples include measures of accuracy, reliability, timeliness, performance, behaviour, delivery, after-sales services, documentation, and appearance. These measures are 'internal' measures. Consumer satisfaction or other customer data should not be included in responses to this item.
(2) Results reported in Item 6.1 should reflect the key product and service features determined in Item 7.1, and be fully consistent with the key quality requirements for products and services described in the Overview.

6.2 Business Process, Operational, and Support Service Quality Results *(50pts.)*

Summarize trends in quality improvement and current quality levels for business processes, operations, and support services.

Areas to address
a. trends and current levels for the most important measures of the

quality and effectiveness of business processes, operations, and support services.

b. comparison with industry averages, industry leaders, and world leaders.

Notes:

(1) Key measures for business processes, operations, and support services are the set of principal measurable characteristics that represent quality and effectiveness in company operations in meeting requirements of customers and of other company units. Examples include measures of accuracy, timeliness, and effectiveness. Measures include error rates, defect rates, lead times, cycle times, and use of manpower, materials, energy, and capital as reflected in indicators such as repeat services, utilization rates, and waste.

(2) The results reported in Item 6.2 derive from quality improvement activities described in Category 5 and Item 1.4 if appropriate. R esponses should reflect relevance to the company's principal quality objectives and should also demonstrate the breadth of improvement results throughout all operations and work units.

6.3 Supplier Quality Results *(40pts.)*

Summarize trends and levels in quality of suppliers and services furnished by other companies; compare the company's supplier quality with that of competitors and with key benchmarks.

Areas to address

a. trends and current levels for the most important indicators of supplier quality.

b. comparison of the company's supplier quality with that of competitors and/or with benchmarks. Such comparisons could include industry averages, industry leaders, world leaders, principal competitors in the company's key markets, and appropriate benchmarks. Describe the bases for comparisons.

Note:

The results reported in Item 6.3 derive from quality improvement activities described in Item 5.7. Results should be broken down by major groupings of suppliers and reported using the principal quality indicators described in Item 5.7.

7.0 CUSTOMER SATISFACTION (300 pts.)

The *Customer Satisfaction* category examines the company's knowledge of the customer, overall customer service systems, responsiveness, and its ability to meet requirements and expectations. Also examined are current levels and trends in customer satisfaction.

7.1 Determining Customer Requirements and Expectations *(30pts.)*
Describe how the company determines current and future customer requirements and expectations.

Areas to address

a. how the company determines current and future requirements and expectations of customers. Include information on: (1) how market segments and customer groups are determined and how customers of competitors and other potential customers are considered; (2) the process for collecting information and data. This should include what information is sought, frequencies of surveys, interviews or other contacts, and how objectivity is assured; (3) how other information and data are cross-compared to support determination of customer requirements and expectations. Such information and data might include performance information on the company's products and services, complaints, gains and losses of customers, customer satisfaction, and competitors' performance.

b. process for determining product and service features and the relative importance of these features to customers and/or customer groups.

c. how the company evaluates and improves its processes for determining customer requirements and expectations as well as the key product and service features.

Notes:

(1) Products and services may be sold to end users by intermediaries such as retail stores or dealers. Thus, determining customer groups should take into account both the end users and the intermediaries.

(2) Product and service features refer to all important characteristics of products and services experienced by the customers throughout the overall purchase and ownership experiences. This includes any factors that bear upon customer preference or customer view of quality – for example, those features that enhance them or differentiate them from competing offerings.

(3) An applicant may choose to describe its offerings, part of its offerings, or certain of its activities as products or services irrespective of the SIC classification of the company. Such descriptions should then be consistent throughout the Application Report.

7.2 Customer Relationship Management *(50pts.)*
Describe how the company provides effective management of its relationship with its customers and uses information gained from customers to improve products and services as well as its customer relationship management practices.

Areas to address

a. means for ensuring easy access for customers to seek assistance and to comment. Describe types of contact, such as telephone, personal, and written, and how the company maintains easy access for each type of contact.

b. follow-up with customers on products and services to determine satisfaction with recent transactions and to seek data and information for improvement.

c. how the following are addressed for customer-contact personnel: (1) selection factor for customer-contact jobs; (2) career path; (3) special training to include: knowledge of products and services, listening to customers, soliciting comment from customers, how to anticipate and handle special problems or failures, and skills in customer retention; (4) empowerment and decision making; (5) attitude and morale determination; (6) recognition and reward; and (7) attrition.

d. how the company provides technology and logistics support for customer-contact personnel to enable them to provide reliable and responsive services.

e. how the company analyses key customer-related data and information to assess costs and market consequences for policy development, planning, and resource allocation.

f. principal factors the company uses to evaluate its customer relationship management, such as response accuracy, timeliness, and customer satisfaction with contacts. Describe how the factors or indicators are used to improve training, technology, or customer-oriented management practices.

Notes:

(1) Other key aspects of customer relationship management are addressed in Items 7.3, 7.4, and 7.5.

(2) Item 7.2c addresses important human resource management requirements specifically for customer-contact personnel. This is included in Item 7.2 for special emphasis and coherence.

7.3 Customer Service Standards *(20pts.)*

Describe the company's standards governing the direct contact between its employees and customers and how these standards are set and modified.

Areas to address

a. how well-defined service standards to meet customer requirements are set. List and briefly describe the company's most important customer service standards.

b. how standards requirements and key standards information are deployed to company units that support customer-contact personnel.

Briefly describe how the company ensures that the support provided by these company units is effective and timely.

c. how service standards are tracked, evaluated, and improved. Describe the role of customer-contact personnel in evaluating and improving standards.

Note:

Service standards are objectively measurable levels of performance that define quality for the overall service or for a part of a service. Examples include measures of response time, problem resolution time, accuracy, and completeness.

7.4 Commitment to Customers *(15pts.)*

Describe the company's commitments to customers on its explicit and implicit promises underlying its products and services.

Areas to address

a. types of commitments the company makes to promote trust and confidence in its products, services, and relationships. Include how the company ensures that these commitments: (1) address the principal concerns of customers; (2) are free from conditions that might weaken customer confidence; and (3) are understandable.

b. how improvements in the quality of the company's products and services over the past three years have been translated into stronger commitments. Compare commitments with those of competing companies.

Note:

Commitments may include product and service guarantees, product warranties, and other understandings with the customer, expressed or implied.

7.5 Complaint Resolution for Quality Improvement *(25pts.)*

Describe how the company handles complaints, resolves them, and uses complaint information for quality improvement and for prevention of recurrence of problems.

Areas to address

a. how the company ensures that formal and informal complaints and feedback given to different company units are aggregated for overall evaluation and use wherever appropriate throughout the company.

b. how the company ensures that complaints are resolved promptly and effectively. Include: (1) trends and levels in indicators of response time; and (2) trends in per cent of complaints resolved on first contact with customer-contact personnel.

c. how complaints are analysed to determine underlying causes and how the findings are translated into improvements. This translation may lead to improvements such as in processes, service standards, training of customer-contact personnel, and information to customers to help them make more effective use of products and/or services.

d. key indicators and methods the company uses to evaluate and improve its complaint-related processes. Describe how indicators and methods address effectiveness, response time improvement, and translation of findings into improvements.

Notes:

(1) A major purpose of aggregation of complaint information is to ensure overall evaluation for policy development, planning, training, and resource allocation. However, this does not imply that complaint resolution and quality improvement should await aggregation or that resolution and improvement are necessarily centralized within a company.

(2) Trends and current levels in complaints are requested in Item 7.7.

7.6 Determining Customer Satisfaction *(20pts.)*

Describe the company's methods for determining customer satisfaction, how satisfaction information is used in quality improvement, and how methods for determining customer satisfaction are improved.

Areas to address

a. how the company determines customer satisfaction for customer groups. Address: (1) brief description of market segments and customer groups; and (2) the process for determining customer satisfaction for customer groups. Include what information is sought, frequency of surveys, interviews or other contacts, and how objectivity is assured. Describe how the company sets the customer satisfaction measurement scale to adequately capture key information that accurately reflects customer preference.

b. how customer satisfaction relative to competitors is determined.

c. how customer satisfaction data are analysed and compared with other customer satisfaction indicators such as complaints and gains and losses of customers. Describe how such comparisons are used to improve customer satisfaction determination.

d. how the company evaluates and improves its overall methods and measurement scales used in determining customer satisfaction and customer satisfaction relative to competitors.

Notes:

(1) Information sought in determining customer satisfaction may include specific product and services features and the relative importance of

these features to customers, thus suppplementing information sought in determining customer requirements and expectations.

(2) The customer satisfaction measurement scale may include both numerical designators and the descriptors assigned to them. An effective scale is one that provides the company with accurate information about specific product and services features and about the customers' likely market behaviours.

7.7 Customer Satisfaction Results *(70pts.)*

Summarize trends in the company's consumer satisfaction and in indicators of adverse customer response.

Areas to address

a. trends and current levels in indicators of customer satisfaction for products and services. Segment these results by customer groups, as appropriate.

b. trends and current levels in major adverse indicators. Adverse indicators include complaints, claims, refunds, recalls, returns, repeat services, litigation, replacements, downgrades, repairs, warranty costs, and warranty work. If the company has received any sanctions under regulation or contract over the past three years, include such information in this item. Briefly describe how sanctions were resolved or current status.

7.8 Customer Satisfaction Comparison *(70pts.)*

Compare the company's customer satisfaction results and recognition with those of competitors that provide similar products and services.

Areas to address

a. comparison of customer satisfaction results. Such comparisons should be made with principal competitors in the company's key markets, industry averages, industry leaders, and world leaders.

b. surveys, competitive awards, recognition, and ratings by independent organizations, including customers. Briefly describe surveys, awards, recognition, and ratings. Include how quality and quality attributes are considered as factors in the evaluations of these independent organizations.

c. trends in gaining or losing customers and in customer and customer account retention. Briefly summarize gains and losses of customers. including those gained from or lost to competitors. Address customer groups or market segments, as appropriate.

d. trends in gaining and losing market share relative to major competitors, domestic and foreign. Briefly explain significant changes in terms of quality comparisons and quality trends.

Appendix 3 BS 5750: Quality manual appraisal for production industries

ISO 9001/2:1987 EN 29001/2:1987 BS 5750:Parts 1/2:1987

Company name: _____

Quality Assurance Representative: _____

Date: _____

The purpose of this publication is to enable you to undertake a self-appraisal of your quality documentation. It is not intended to cover every aspect of BS 5750 requirements but function as an aid and guide to management in assessing the adequacy of your documented system.

The questions should be answered in so far as the functions described apply to your firm's scope of activity by identifying where your documented system meets the requirement. Alternatively make a qualified comment if you consider the question not applicable.

Quality manual appraisal for production industries

ISO 9001/2:1987 EN 29001/2:1987 BS 5750:Parts 1/2:1987

ISO 9001 EN 29001 Part 1	ISO 9002 EN 29002 Part 2	Requirements of ISO 9000/EN 29000/ BS 5750	Quality Manual Reference or State N/A*	Comments
4.1	4.1	**Management Responsibility**		
4.1.1	4.1.1	Quality Policy		
		Where are the company policies and procedures for controllng quality set out?		
		How are the policies and procedures made known to and understood by all staff?		
4.1.2	4.1.2	Organization		
4.1.2.1	4.1.2.1	Responsibility and Authority		
		Where is the management structure, the tasks, responsibilities and authority of officials documented?		
		Where are responsibilities and channels for identification, recording and solving of product quality problems defined?		
4.1.2.2	4.1.2.2	Verification resources and personnel		
		Where is it specified that personnel are given the necessary training and authority to perform their function		
		Where are the procedures to cover verification activities eg. inspection, test, review and monitoring?		
4.1.2.3	4.1.2.3	Management representative		
		Where is it documented that there is a representative who has the responsibility and authority for implementing and maintaining the quality system?		

*N/A = Not applicable

ISO 9001 EN 29001 Part 1	ISO 9002 EN 29002 Part 2	Requirements of ISO 9000/EN 29000/ BS 5750	Quality Manual Reference or State N/A*	Comments
4.1.3	4.1.3	Management Review		
		Where does the documentation define a senior management review process, including how and by whom the review will be conducted, the records will be maintained and how data will be used		
4.2	4.2	**Quality System**		
		Where is it stipulated that a documented quality system shall be prepared to meet the requirements of the standard?		
		Where are the procedures for identifying the role of the quality department in managing and ensuring that all aspects of the system comply with the standard?		
4.3	4.3	**Contract Review**		
		Where is the documented procedure for examining and reviewing contract requirements to ensure that they are adequately defined?		
		Does this procedure cover the resolution of differences from the tender and ensure that there is sufficient capability to meet all the requirements of the contract?		

*N/A = Not applicable

ISO 9001 EN 29001 Part 1	ISO 9002 EN 29002 Part 2	Requirements of ISO 9000/EN 29000/ BS 5750	Quality Manual Reference or State N/A*	Comments
4.4	**N/A**	**Design Control**		
4.4.1	N/A	General		
		Where are the procedures that define the control of the various aspects of the design function eg. code of design practice and procedures, the evaluation of new materials, reliability, value engineering etc?		
4.4.2	N/A	Design and development planning		
		Where are the procedures that define the responsibility for the design activity including the methods of planning and means of updating these plans and activities as the design evolves?		
4.4.2.1		Activity assignment		
		Where are the planning procedures that prescribe the assignment of activities to personnel. Are personnel equipped with adequate resources?		
4.4.2.2	N/A	Organizational and technical interfaces		
		Where is the design department organization documented, and are interfaces between groups within and external to the design group identified eg. is data supplied to purchasing, manufacturing and inspection functions so that contractual requirements can be met?		
		Is there a formal review procedure to ensure that contract design requirements can be complied with?		

*N/A = Not applicable

ISO 9001 EN 29001 Part 1	ISO 9002 EN 29002 Part 2	Requirements of ISO 9000/EN 29000/ BS 5750	Quality Manual Reference or State N/A*	Comments
4.4.3	N/A	Design Input		
		Where are the procedures that ensure timely identification and acquisition of materials, bought out items, controls, processes, inspection equipment, fixtures, tooling and skills?		
		Is there a mechanism for resolving any conflicting or ambiguous requirements?		
4.4.4	N/A	Design Output		
		Where are the procedures which define the design output requirements?		
		Do they ensure design input has been met and contain/reference acceptance criteria?		
		Do they address any appropriate regulatory requirements?		
		Is there a mechanism for identifying characteristics crucial to the safe and proper function of the design?		
4.4.5	N/A	Design Verification		
		Where are plans for verifying the design defined and is such activity assigned to competent personnel?		
		Are there procedures for the holding and recording of formal design reviews?		
		Are there procedures for the control of tests, trials and demonstrations?		
		Is there a means of review for new design compared to similar proven design?		

*N/A = Not applicable

ISO 9001 EN 29001 Part 1	ISO 9002 EN 29002 Part 2	Requirements of ISO 9000/EN 29000/ BS 5750	Quality Manual Reference or State N/A*	Comments
4.4.6	N/A	Design Changes		
		Where are the procedures which cover the proposal, approval and implementation of design changes including those resulting from feedback information?		
4.5	**4.4**	**Document Control**		
4.5.1	4.4.1	Document Approval and Use		
		Identify the procedures which give a clear and precise definition of responsibilities for issue and revision of drawings, documents, manuals, instructions etc.		
		Where does the system ensure all pertinent issues of documents will be available at the necessary locations and provide for removal of obsolete documents from all points of issue or use?		
4.5.2	4.4.2	Document changes/ modifications		
		Where is the mechanism for the review and change of documentation prescribed?		
		How is the nature of a change to a document defined?		
		Is there a master list for all drawings, documentation and forms used?		
4.6	**4.5**	**Purchasing**		
4.6.1	4.5.1	General		
		Identify the procedures for the purchasing of all products and services necessary to meet the specified requirements.		

*N/A = Not applicable

ISO 9001 EN 29001 Part 1	ISO 9002 EN 29002 Part 2	Requirements of ISO 9000/EN 29000/ BS 5750	Quality Manual Reference or State N/A*	Comments
4.6.2	4.5.2	Assessment of sub-contractors		
		Identify the procedures to cover the selection and control of sub-contractors; do they detail the records to be maintained?		
4.6.3	4.5.3	Purchasing Data		
		Identify the procedures that clearly prescribe the data to be entered on purchasing documents.		
		Are there procedures for the review and approval of purchasing documents for adequacy of specified require-ments prior to release?		
		Is it prescribed that purchasing documents should make reference to drawings, specifica-tions, quality standards and contract require-ments as necessary?		
4.6.4	4.5.4	Verification of purchased product		
		How does the system acknowledge the right of a company represen-tative to verify at source that the purchased product conforms to contract requirements?		
4.7	4.6	**Purchaser Supplied Product**		
		Identify the procedures for the verification, storage and maintenance of purchaser supplied products?		
		Is there a mechanism for recording and reporting such products which are lost, damaged or unsuitable for use?		

*N/A = Not applicable

ISO 9001 EN 29001 Part 1	ISO 9002 EN 29002 Part 2	Requirements of ISO 9000/EN 29000/ BS 5750	Quality Manual Reference or State N/A*	Comments
4.8	4.7	**Product Identification and Traceability**		
		Where appropriate do procedures exist for identifying product through all stages of production, delivery and installation?		
4.9	4.8	**Process Control**		
4.9.1	4.8.1	General		
		Do documented work instructions define the manner of production and installation?		
		Do procedures exist for controlling, reviewing and updating these work instructions?		
		Are workmanship standards defined and documented?		
		Is the monitoring and control of suitable processes defined together with product characterization during production and installation?		
		Does the system ensure that the processes and equipment used have the required capability?		
4.9.2	4.8.2	Special Processes		
		How are any special processes identified and do procedures exist to cover their control and monitoring?		
		Is it stipulated that records shall be maintained for special processes, equipment and personnel as appropriate?		

*N/A = Not applicable

ISO 9001 EN 29001 Part 1	ISO 9002 EN 29002 Part 2	Requirements of ISO 9000/EN 29000/ BS 5750	Quality Manual Reference or State N/A*	Comments
4.10	**4.9**	**Inspection and Testing**		
4.10.1	4.9.1	Receiving Inspection and Testing		
		Where are the procedures which define how material is to be inspected or verified as conforming to requirements?		
		Is there a defined system for the clear identification of released, rejected, quarantined or unchecked incoming materials?		
4.10.2	4.9.2	In-process inspection and testing		
		Where are the procedures which define in-process inspection and testing stages and requirements?		
		Are methods of process monitoring and control to establish product conformance defined?		
		Do procedures cover the holding and identification of product pending clearance through inspection or test.		
4.10.3	4.9.3	Final Inspection and Testing		
		Identify the documented procedures for final inspection and testing. Do they ensure that all previous inspection/testing meets the defined acceptance criteria?		
		Do procedures preclude the despatch of product until all the activities specified have been completed?		

*N/A = Not applicable

ISO 9001 EN 29001 Part 1	ISO 9002 EN 29002 Part 2	Requirements of ISO 9000/EN 29000/ BS 5750	Quality Manual Reference or State N/A*	Comments
4.10.4	4.9.4	Inspection and test records		
		How does the system prescribe the retention of all relevant records to show that the product has passed inspection/ test with defined acceptance criteria?		
4.11	4.10	**Inspection Measuring and Test Equipment**		
		How do the procedures define the facilities and environments for calibration, handling, control, storage and maintenance of all the necessary measuring and test equipment?		
		Are there documented procedures (where applicable) which are used for calibrating all equipment and standards which include method of calibration acceptance criteria and action to be taken when results are unsatisfactory?		
		Do procedures ensure that calibrated equipment is suitably identified to show its calibration status?		
		Are the accuracies of all standards traceable to national or international standards?		
		Are there procedures to safeguard inspection measuring and test facilities for adjustments which would invalidate the calibration setting?		
		Do procedures exist to ensure that, where test hardware and software is used for inspection, it is capable of verifying the acceptability of product prior to release?		

*N/A = Not applicable

ISO 9001 EN 29001 Part 1	ISO 9002 EN 29002 Part 2	Requirements of ISO 9000/EN 29000/ BS 5750	Quality Manual Reference or State N/A*	Comments
		Do these procedures define the extent and frequency of such checks?		
4.12	4.11	**Inspection and Test Status**		
		Where are the documented procedures for identifying the inspection and test status of product throughout the production and installation process?		
		Is the authority for the release on conforming product defined?		
4.13	4.12	**Control of Non-conforming Product**		
		Identifying the procedures for controlling nonconforming product.		
		Do they cover identification, documentation, evaluation, segregation, disposition and notification to functions concerned?		
4.13.1	4.12.1	Nonconformity review and disposition		
		Identify the procedures which define the responsibility and authority for review and disposition of nonconforming product.		
		Are there procedures requiring repaired and reworked products to be reinspected?		
		Are records of meetings to dispose of scrap and rework material maintained?		
		Do procedures cater for customer concessions when required in contract?		

*N/A = Not applicable

ISO 9001 EN 29001 Part 1	ISO 9002 EN 29002 Part 2	Requirements of ISO 9000/EN 29000/ BS 5750	Quality Manual Reference or State N/A*	Comments
4.14	4.13	**Corrective Action**		
		Are there documented procedures for the investigation of the causes of nonconforming product or service and do they include corrective actions to prevent recurrence?		
		Does the system ensure that all processes, work operations, concessions, quality records, service reports and customer complaints are analysed to detect and eliminate potential causes of nonconforming product or service?		
		Is there a procedure for monitoring corrective actions to ensure they are effective?		
		Is provision made for the recording of procedural changes resulting from corrective action?		
		Is there a mechanism for initiating preventative actions to deal with problems on an associated risk level basis?		
4.15	4.14	**Handling, Storage, Packaging and Delivery**		
4.15.1	4.14.1	General		
		Identify the procedures for handling, storage, packaging and delivery of product.		
4.15.2	4.14.2	Handling		
		Where are the handling methods prescribed which prevent damage or deterioration of product?		

*N/A = Not applicable

ISO 9001 EN 29001 Part 1	ISO 9002 EN 29002 Part 2	Requirements of ISO 9000/EN 29000/ BS 5750	Quality Manual Reference or State N/A*	Comments
4.15.3	4.14.3	Storage		
		Identify the procedures for controlling receipt and issue of product from stock rooms or other such secure storage areas.		
		Are there procedures for identification/ segregation of product and do they cover the assessment of its condition at defined intervals?		
4.15.4	4.14.4	Packaging		
		How are the processes of packaging, preservation and marking defined and controlled?		
4.15.5	4.14.5	Delivery		
		How does the documented system cover the protection of the quality of product after final inspection and during transit to final destination?		
4.16	4.15	**Quality Records**		
		Identify the procedures for the maintenance, identification, collection, indexing, filing, storage and disposition of quality records – such records being those which demonstrate the maintenance and achievement of the required quality and effective operation of the quality system.		
		Does the system ensure that such records are satisfactorily stored and readily retrievable and is their retention period stipulated?		

*N/A = Not applicable

ISO 9001 EN 29001 Part 1	ISO 9002 EN 29002 Part 2	Requirements of ISO 9000/EN 29000/ BS 5750	Quality Manual Reference or State N/A*	Comments
4.17	4.16	**Internal Quality Audits**		
		Identify the procedure for internal quality audits.		
		Does this cover scheduling, method of audit and follow-up actions to be taken?		
		Are results of audits brought to the attention of personnel responsible in the area audited?		
		Do procedures require such personnel to initiate and document the corrective action taken?		
		Are audits carried out by personnel independent of the department/ area being audited?		
4.18	4.17	**Training**		
		Identify the procedures that define the training needs and provisions made for the training of all personnel performing activities affecting quality?		
		How are records of training maintained?		
		Are methods defined for the qualification of personnel for special processes and operations such as welding, NDT etc?		
4.19	N/A	**Servicing**		
		If appropriate, identify the documented procedures for performing and verifying that servicing meets the specified requiremens.		

*N/A = Not applicable

ISO 9001 EN 29001 Part 1	ISO 9002 EN 29002 Part 2	Requirements of ISO 9000/EN 29000/ BS 5750	Quality Manual Reference or State N/A*	Comments
4.20	4.18	**Statistical Techniques**		
		If appropriate, identify the procedures which cover statistical techniques for verifying the acceptability of process capability and product characterization.		

*N/A = Not applicable

Index